The Age of de Valera

The Age of de Valera

by Joseph Lee
and Gearóid Ó Tuathaigh

Picture research by Carmel Duignan
Captions and Preface by Peter Feeney

DUBLIN: WARD RIVER PRESS
in association with
RADIO TELEFÍS ÉIREANN

First published 1982 by
Ward River Press Ltd.,
Knocksedan House,
Swords, Co. Dublin, Ireland.

ISBN 0 907085 33 4 paperback
0 907085 34 2 hardback

Cover illustration and drawings of de Valera by Don Farrell
Designed by Steven Hope
Typeset in Linotype Palatino by Leaders, Swords
Printed by Cahill Printers Limited, East Wall Road, Dublin 3

The Age of de Valera

Script:	Joseph Lee and Gearóid Ó Tuathaigh
Narrator:	Barry McGovern
Film Editor:	Gerry Fallon
Film Cameraman:	Ken Murphy
Film Sound:	Pat Murray
Film Dubbing:	Terry Gough
Electrical Supervisor:	Kevin O'Toole
Assistant Film Cameraman:	Alastair Neely
Assistant Film Editors:	Bill Forde and Declan Lowney
Graphic Designer:	Don Farrell
Special Advisor:	Dermot Keogh
Theme Music:	Bill Whelan
Production Assistant:	Carmel Duignan
Producer/Director:	Peter Feeney

Contents

Preface

There are constraints on television history which do not apply to any other form of historical research. Primary amongst these is the limitation imposed by having to illustrate visually all the subjects raised in the script. In some cases this is an intellectual problem – what illustrations can one use to further an argument on sovereignty? But more often than not the problem is the limited availability of film from the past.

To our shame, Ireland has no national film archive. Most of the film shot in Ireland in the first half of this century is deposited in libraries in England. Film makers are always selective in the subjects they choose to film. By and large, political events were well covered by the cinema newsreel cameramen in the 1920s and 1930s. But if a producer is looking for material to illustrate the everyday lives of ordinary men and women in Ireland, archive film is almost non-existent. A good example of this is emigration. The most common experience for many Irish men and women up to the 1960s was leaving the country to find employment. Yet in our research for the series, we were simply unable to find any film of people boarding ships as they left Ireland.

In preparing "The Age of de Valera" we had the considerable advantage of access to the historical film gathered together and reproduced for the BBC/RTE co-production, Robert Kee's "Ireland – A Television History". This made available, in a usable form, much material which would otherwise have been very difficult to obtain.

During his lifetime, Éamon de Valera aroused the strongest of passions. He was either loved or hated; few were neutral. Inevitably, as the series was being prepared, people asked whether it was for or against de Valera. If one answered that the series was intended to be an objective evaluation of his role in the development of post-independence Ireland, the response was invariably a sceptical raising of eyebrows. In truth, it is inevitable that with the advantage of hindsight, the judgement is bound to be critical. If Éamon de Valera had known what we know today, perhaps he would have made different decisions. But the excessive use of hindsight can lead to bad historical analysis: imposing present-day values and concerns on past events. Such judgements tell us more about the period in which the historical research is done than they do about the period under examination. I hope that the television series and this accompanying book avoid these pitfalls.

A television programme is an ephemeral thing. It is broadcast and it is gone. Recall has only the use of an imperfect memory. Perhaps, in the not too distant future, with the widespread availability of home video recorders, this may no longer be so. But for the moment, a printed book is the best way of ensuring the permanent accessibility of a television series. With a subject as interesting and as controversial as "The Age of de Valera", this cannot but be useful for anyone trying to understand the last sixty years of Irish history. The problems raised in this series are historical problems – the partition of Ireland, the kind of society we want in Ireland, the role of our Gaelic past – but they are problems which we still have with us. If we understand our past we can understand our present.

A television series is a product of many skilled men

and women working as a team. Within RTE, I would like to acknowledge the important contributions of Carmel Duignan, Muiris Mac Conghail, Seán Ó Mórdha, Gerry Fallon, Ken Murphy, Don Farrell and the staff of the RTE libraries. Outside of RTE, the two authors of this book scripted the television series. A good series depends on imaginative, provocative scriptwriting, and in this case RTE has been well served. Other historians who assisted by their advice and encouragement include Dermot Keogh, Paul Bew, Deirdre McMahon, T. Ryle Dwyer, Eamon Phoenix and David Harkness. A word of thanks ought to go to all the people who agreed to be interviewed for the series. Trying to recall events that happened up to sixty years ago in front of cameras and lights cannot have been easy for many people. The generous access to the de Valera private family film, made available by Professor Éamonn de Valera, is clearly evident in the television series.

Finally, one of the pleasures in producing the series was reading and, in some cases, re-reading many books about twentieth century Irish history. Other than the two most reliable reference books, *Éamon de Valera* by the Earl of Longford and T. P. O'Neill, and *Speeches and Statements of Éamon de Valera 1917-73* edited by Maurice Moynihan, three books stand in my memory. Of these, the titles of two explain their contents: *The Evolution of Irish Nationalist Politics* by Tom Garvin, and *Ireland: A Social and Cultural History 1922-79* by Terence Brown. The third book is *Voices and the Sound of Drums*, by Patrick Shea. This is a beautiful account of conflicting loyalties in which the author describes his childhood as a Catholic RIC man's son during the War of Independence, and later as one of the few Catholics to rise to the top of the Northern Ireland Civil Service.

Peter Feeney

Introduction

At various times in Irish history – as in the history of every people – there have been individuals whose impact, influence and personality have set them apart from their contemporaries and earned for them the special consideration of historians and of all those intent on understanding the great impersonal forces and the decisive events which shape a country's history. In modern Ireland such a man was Éamon de Valera, a man whose towering presence – like that of O'Connell or Parnell before him (and these are the only figures who stand comparison with him in the modern era) – presides over a great part of the story of modern Ireland in the first half of the twentieth century. The sole surviving commandant of the 1916 rising; the Príomh-Aire/President of the First Dáil; the founder and long-time leader of the most powerful and consistently successful political party ever in Irish history (if not, indeed, among the most successful in modern Europe); Head of Government for over twenty of the state's first thirty seven years of existence, and afterwards head of state (Uachtarán) for a further fourteen years – the name de Valera evokes an immediate and powerful response across the full spectrum of Irish political opinion, from unswerving loyalty and unmeasured devotion on the one hand, to deep-seated bitterness and hostility on the other. Furthermore, for friend and foe alike, to the outside world the name de Valera was almost synonymous with Ireland thoughout the middle decades of this century, if not indeed right up to his death in 1975. Clearly, then, the story of Ireland in the twentieth century, the story of our times, as it were, cannot be comprehended without coming to grips with the influence and achievements, the ideas and objectives, the life and the legacy of Éamon de Valera.

This book is based on the television series *The Age of de Valera*, broadcast by RTÉ in the autumn of 1982, to coincide with the centenary of de Valera's birth. Chapters 2, 3, 4 and 5 are substantively the essays on which the five programmes of the series were based. However, for the purposes of publication in book form, these essays have been re-written and considerably expanded. The book also contains extra material, which could not be easily accommodated in the format of a television series. The illustrations are drawn from the materials used in the series as broadcast. Footnotes are not included, but a brief bibliographical note indicates the most useful sources of information and quotation.

The intention of the book, as of the series, is not to provide a straight biography of de Valera, still less a conventional "course of Irish history" between 1882 and 1975. The authors sought to identify and to offer an analysis of a number of key characteristics of, and developments in, Irish society during the period of de Valera's political ascendancy. Thus, the enterprise was conceived as a series of essays in interpretation, with the general concept of sovereignty as the controlling theme. This seemed an admissible way of structuring the analysis, as sovereignty – in all its manifold aspects – was the most obsessive, as well as being in many ways the most integrating force in de Valera's ideal of Ireland, as a political, social and cultural entity.

Chapters 1, 2 and 5 are Ó Tuathaigh's responsibility; chapters 3 and 4 are Lee's.

Chapter 1

Biographical Profile

Éamon de Valera was born in the New York Nursery and Childs Hospital in Lexington Avenue on 14 October 1882. He was, in fact, registered as George, but baptised as Edward (which he later translated to Éamon after his conversion to the cause of revival of the Irish language). His father was Juan de Valera (son of a Spanish sugar trader), who had studied to be a sculptor; but in consequence of an injury to his eyes and generally indifferent health he had reverted to teaching music. In September 1881 Juan de Valera had married another exile, Kate Coll from Knockmore, near Bruree, Co. Limerick, a young girl who had emigrated to America two years earlier. Juan de Valera's health did not improve, despite treatment, and in the spring of 1885 he died while his infant son was only two. Under the circumstances, Kate Coll decided that her son would be better off at home in Ireland. Thus it happened that Éamon de Valera returned to Knockmore in 1885 (travelling with his uncle), to the labourer's cottage in which he was to spend his early youth.

De Valera attended Bruree national school and, despite the fact that he was not the best attender, he showed clear all-round ability. As the future seemed to hold nothing better for him than a school monitorship (i.e. an untrained and underpaid assistant teacher) or the hard life of a labourer, he became restless and anxious to return to America. Eventually, however, his academic ability brought improved opportunities. After a spell at

Éamon de Valera's father, Juan. He died when Éamon was in his second year.

Éamon de Valera's mother, Catherine (Kate) Coll who, as a young Irish emigrant in New York, married Juan de Valera, of Spanish origin. It was destined to be a very short marriage.

the CBS in Charleville, de Valera won an exhibition to Blackrock College (where, now aged sixteen, he originally intended becoming a priest).

These early Bruree years, however, were crucial to de Valera's psychological development and to his own self-perception in later life. His Spanish name was frequently to expose him to the jibes of his political opponents at various times throughout his career, the claim being that he wasn't really Irish and did not fully understand "the Irish mind." The years in Bruree always gave de Valera

16

his most effective weapon in rebutting this charge. His boyhood years reassured him that he was of "the plain people of Ireland," and indeed was closer to the grass-roots than many of those Catholic bourgeois critics of his who had spent their comfortable youth and early man-hood in lecture halls and debating societies. It was in answering one such jibe at his "foreigness" (this time in the *Freeman's Journal*) that he made his celebrated (but frequently misunderstood) assertion in January 1921:

> I have been brought up amongst the Irish people. I was reared in a labourer's cottage here in Ireland. I have not lived solely amongst the intellectuals. The first fifteen years of my life that formed my character were lived amongst the Irish people down in Limerick; therefore I know what I am talking about; and when-ever I wanted to know what the Irish people wanted I had only to examine my own heart and it told me straight off what the Irish people wanted.

Solid all-round performance at Blackrock and a special aptitude for mathematics saw de Valera matriculate and complete two university examinations in the Royal University. The offer of a job as senior master in mathe-matics in Rockwell College was quickly accepted, and brought many rewards. But it left little time for prepar-ation for the final degree examination, and de Valera finally had to be satisfied with a pass degree. He was disappointed with his degree and began to fear that he would go to seed if he remained much longer at Rockwell. So he returned to Dublin, first to Belvedere College, and then (in September 1906) as Professor of Mathematics at Carysfort College, Blackrock. He maintained his interest in mathematics and in metaphysics and kept himself

The house outside Bruree, Co. Limerick where Éamon de Valera was raised by his uncle and his grandmother. His view that he instinctively knew what the Irish people wanted was based on his childhood in Bruree. From his mid-teens onward he lived almost continuously in Dublin.

busy with the part-time teaching of students doing exams at the Royal University. This extra income was badly missed when the establishment of the National University of Ireland in 1909 brought de Valera's "moonlighting" to an end.

By this time, however, de Valera was becoming more and more involved in what was to be one of the most enduring passions of his life, his involvement in the movement for the revival of the Irish language. De Valera joined the Gaelic League in 1908, and became an enthusiastic and life-long convert. Among his teachers

Éamon de Valera at four years. With an uncle and a grandmother for step-parents and a foreign-sounding name, life cannot have been easy for the little boy.

Éamon de Valera aged twelve, with a bright educational career before him if his family's poverty could be overcome. Assistance from church and state came to his aid.

at the League was one four years his senior, named Sinéad Flanagan. They fell in love and were married in January 1910. The Gaelic League was only one of the agencies which sharpened de Valera's national consciousness (as with many other idealists of that generation) in the critical years 1910-14 during which the Home Rule bill became a crucial issue in British politics. De Valera joined the Irish Volunteers at their inaugural meeting in 1913, and when the Liberal government put

the implementation of the Home Rule Bill on the long finger (under pressure from the Unionists in Ulster and in Britain) de Valera moved firmly into the separatist camp in Ireland. He commanded the Boland's Mills garrison during the 1916 rising. After the surrender he was sentenced to death, but subsequently had the sentence commuted. In prison (in Dartmouth and elsewhere in England) de Valera emerged not only as a leader of considerable personal magnetism but also as a major presence for unity and conciliation between different nationalist elements (for example, he was scrupulous in showing respect to Eoin Mac Néill, despite Mac Néill's controversial role in cancelling the manoeuvres intended to signal the beginning of the rising).

De Valera was released from prison in June 1917 and was promptly elected Sinn Féin deputy for East Clare, defeating Patrick Lynch, KC, by 5,010 votes to 2,135. At the Sinn Féin Árd-Fheis in October 1917 de Valera was elected President of the reconstructed party, and at the end of the same month he was elected President of the Irish Volunteers. Clearly, then, by spring 1918 he was the acknowledged head of the separatist movement in Ireland. When the British government proposed to extend conscription to Ireland in early 1918, de Valera led the broad, and ultimately successful, opposition to this proposal. On 17 May 1918 de Valera was arrested and deported for internment to England, where he was to remain up to February 1919. During internment he was returned unopposed for East Clare in the general election

At Blackrock College Éamon de Valera (second from right in front row) was a contented pupil. He retained his affection for the Holy Ghost order throughout his life.

During his schooldays, Éamon de Valera considered becoming a priest. Afterwards, he opted for a career as a teacher of mathematics. At Blackrock he showed little interest in politics; his later enthusiasm for the Irish language was to lead him into political activity.

of December 1918 (he was also returned for East Mayo). He did not attend the first historic meeting of Dáil Éireann in January 1919 where the assembled deputies ratified the independent Irish Republic. After his dramatic escape from Lincoln Jail on 3 February 1919 de Valera returned briefly to Ireland and was elected Príomh-Aire of the Dáil. Early in June 1919 he travelled to the USA, where he was to remain (seeking diplomatic, financial and political support for an independent Ireland) until December 1920. On his return to Ireland de Valera resumed his role as President. While his political leadership was not contested, it was, perhaps, inevitable that several of those who had become prominent in his absence (especially in the military campaign) should feel uneasy at his return.

By the (British) Government of Ireland Act, 1920, two parliaments (with defined and limited powers) were to be set up for Southern (26-county) and for Northern (6-county) Ireland. In May 1921 elections were held throughout Ireland for these assemblies, the exercise being regarded by the Republican government as elections for the Second Dáil. In the event, Sinn Féin candidates were returned unopposed in 124 of the 128 seats in the 26 counties (the remaining four being filled unopposed by Unionists in the University of Dublin constituency). In the 6 counties of Northern Ireland Unionists won 40 of the 52 seats, with de Valera (elected for Down) being among the dozen Nationalists and Sinn Féiners returned. Within a month the parliament of

Éamon de Valera on bicycle at left. He was a talented and enthusiastic student and sportsman.

Éamon de Valera's marriage to Sinéad Ní Fhlannagáin took place in 1910. They had met each other at a Gaelic League class, where Sinéad was the teacher, Éamon the pupil. A handsome couple brought together by a shared interest in the Irish language, their union was to last for over sixty years.

Northern Ireland began to function. In the South, however, the verdict of the general election was reinforced by growing evidence that world public opinion, particularly in the USA and Britain, was becoming increasingly insistent that the Anglo-Irish war (the name given to the guerrilla war between the IRA and the British forces – including the Auxiliaries and the Black and Tans – which had been going on since early 1919) should be ended, and an acceptable political settlement reached. Eventually, in July 1921 a truce was arranged, and de Valera journeyed to London for talks with Lloyd George. The talks did not produce an acceptable solution, and de Valera's rejection of the British terms was unanimously endorsed by the Second Dáil in August. Later that month the newly elected Second Dáil unanimously re-elected de Valera as "President of the Irish Republic."

Exploratory negotiations with the British continued, and in late September it was agreed that Irish delegates be sent to a conference in London to see if new terms for a settlement could be agreed. De Valera did not join the delegates for the London talks, which lasted from 11 October to 6 December 1921. (At this time, in November, he was elected to the honorary office of Chancellor of the National University of Ireland, an office he was to hold for the remainder of his life). At the end of the crucial talks in London the delegates finally signed "articles of agreement," by which Ireland (in effect the 26 counties, as Northern Ireland's exclusion from any unitary Irish state was effectively guaranteed, in accordance with the wishes of a local majority) was to be granted a form of dominion status within the British empire, subject to certain conditions, particularly relating to defence.

De Valera found these terms unacceptable, and he led

the opposition to them in the Treaty debates in Dáil Éireann, during the course of which he formulated in detail his own alternative scheme of External Association (incorporated in Document No. 2) which had been maturing in his mind and in his speeches for some time prior to 1921. In the event, however, the Treaty proposals were carried by Dáil Éireann on 7 January 1922, on a vote of 64 to 57. De Valera resigned as President and the bitter divisions on the Treaty terms already revealed in the Dáil began to spread throughout nationalist Ireland. Attempts to prevent an open split foundered on suspicion, misunderstanding and deceit. The general election of June 1922 returned a decided majority in favour of the Treaty (there were 58 pro-Treaty deputies elected, as against 36 anti-Treatyites and 34 others). The war of words had now become a bloody civil war.

During the civil war of 1922-23 de Valera was political leader of the anti-Treaty republican forces, with the title "President of the Republic and Chief Executive of the state". But the initiative and real power lay with the military men rather than with the politicians, despite de Valera's attempts (notably his re-organisation of Sinn Féin in early 1923) to revive the political debate. Finally, in late May 1923 the chief-of-staff of the anti-Treaty forces, Frank Aiken, gave the order to cease fire and dump arms, and de Valera's accompanying message clearly indicated his desire for a cessation of the military struggle and for a resumption of political debate.

However, the years immediately following the civil war were years of frustration and disappointment for de Valera, now in his early forties. He himself was arrested by Free State troops in Ennis on 15 August 1923 during an election campaign, and he spent almost a year in prison (first in Arbour Hill and afterwards in Kilmain-

ham). His release in July 1924 was not followed by any
early improvement in his political prospects. The fiasco
of the Boundary Commission in 1925 served to reinforce
de Valera's hardening conviction that the abstentionist
strategy was a cul-de-sac for the republican movement.
In March 1926, at an extraordinary Árd-Fheis of Sinn
Féin, de Valera proposed a motion:

> That once the admission oaths of the Twenty-six
> County and Six-County assemblies are removed, it
> becomes a question not of principle but of policy
> whether or not Republican representatives should
> attend these assemblies.

This motion was narrowly defeated, and de Valera
resigned the presidency of Sinn Féin. Two months later,
on 16 May 1926, he and his followers founded a new
party, Fianna Fáil.

In August 1927 the Fianna Fáil deputies entered Dáil
Éireann, and de Valera became leader of the Opposition
in the Dáil. Believing that the activities of Fianna Fáil, in
the Dáil and in the country, were not being adequately or
fairly reported, de Valera now resolved to establish a
new newspaper to present the republican point of view.
After a further visit to the USA, lasting from December
1929 to May 1930, de Valera finally launched his newspaper, *The Irish Press,* in September 1931. In the general
election of the following year Fianna Fail won 72 seats
out of a total of 153, and with the support of Labour and
some Independents, de Valera formed his first government. He was thus in his fiftieth year when he
became President of the Executive Council (in effect,
Prime Minister or, as the office was subsequently styled,
Taoiseach) for the first time, and he was to remain in
power for an unbroken period of sixteen years.

The multifarious activities and achievements of these

sixteen years are recounted and analysed elsewhere in this book. That they were eventful years, for de Valera and for the country, can hardly be doubted. A dramatic series of major constitutional changes culminated in the adoption of a new constitution by plebiscite on 1 July 1937 (685, 105 voting in favour, with 526, 945 against). An "economic war" with Britain, based on a dispute over the repayment of the land annuities to Britain, caused considerable economic disruption in Ireland and seriously intensified the kind of problems experienced by all trading nations in the early thirties. Eventually, in 1938, an Anglo-Irish Agreement not only resolved the major economic issues in dispute but also consigned to the control of the Irish state the naval ports which Britain had retained since 1922. On the home front, political excitement was not confined to the seven general elections which took place between 1932 and 1948. The state itself came under serious threat of subversion from several extra-parliamentary movements, the most important of which were the IRA and the right-wing Blueshirt movement of the 1930s. De Valera did not hesitate, despite his own earlier career, to use emergency powers to suppress these various threats. The war years, 1939-45, saw the de Valera government acting with particular vigilance and vigour against the IRA.

The neutrality of the Irish state during the Second World War will always count among de Valera's most notable and most difficult accomplishments in the field of international relations. However, it was neither an abrupt "new departure" nor a retreat into fearful isolation. Throughout the thirties, de Valera had played a prominent role in the League of Nations (being President of the Council and of the Assembly on different occasions). A staunch, but realistic, advocate of international order and the peaceful resolution of disputes between states, de Valera was not afraid to take a firm stand on controversial issues. For example, he urged the admission of Russia to the League of Nations in 1934, supported the sanctions against Italy after its invasion of Abyssinia in 1936, and in 1938 welcomed the Munich Agreement.

The scrupulous maintenance of neutrality during the Second World War caused much resentment in Britain and in some circles in the USA. But it was not based on isolationism. In 1946 de Valera proposed that the Irish state should seek membership of the United Nations. In the event, the opposition of the Soviet Union delayed Ireland's admission until 1955. Again, de Valera participated in the international conference in Paris in 1947 to discuss American aid for the post-war European recovery programme. The importance which he attached to foreign affairs is evidenced by de Valera's decision to retain personally this crucial portfolio throughout the sixteen years up to 1948. Indeed, the burden of work which fell on his shoulders in these years may be gauged by the fact that, notwithstanding this high profile in foreign affairs, de Valera continued to take an active interest in many other aspects of domestic, social and economic policy, and for a short interval (September 1939 to June 1940) held the Education portfolio in addition to being Taoiseach and Minister for External Affairs.

In the general election of February 1948 Fianna Fáil won only 68 seats out of a total of 147. A combination of parties formed a coalition government with John A. Costello as Taoiseach. De Valera became leader of the Opposition for the first time since 1932. Immediately he embarked upon a world tour, to inform international opinion on the partition problem. Far from being weakened, however, partition became even more firmly established as a result of developments in 1949. In that year the government (with John A. Costello as Taoiseach) repealed the External Relations Act of 1936 and declared the state a Republic. In response, the British government passed an Act declaring that in no event would Northern Ireland cease to be part of the United Kingdom without the consent of the Parliament of Northern Ireland. Partition seemed more copper-fastened than ever.

The collapse of the first coalition in 1951 precipitated a general election in which de Valera's Fianna Fáil party gained 69 seats out of 147. With the support of a number of independents, de Valera, now in his sixty-ninth year, became Taoiseach again, though on this occasion he allocated the External Affairs portfolio to Frank Aiken. This minority government was faced with difficult economic problems and only lasted three years. In the general election of 1954 Fianna Fáil's Dáil strength was reduced to 65 (out of 147), and de Valera once more found himself leader of the Opposition. The government of his successor (John A. Costello) soon found itself faced with economic difficulties no less difficult than those which had plagued de Valera's government of 1951-54, and its life was equally short. In the general election of 1957 Fianna Fáil secured 78 seats out of 147, and de Valera, in his seventy-fifth year, began his last term as Taoiseach. This final term was brief, but eventful. It saw the intensification of a new campaign by the IRA against the border, to which de Valera responded with a further dose of emergency legislation (including special powers of arrest and detention without trial). On a brighter note, in 1958 the government launched the First Programme for Economic Expansion (based on T. K.

Whitaker's *Economic Development*). Whatever its short-comings, this programme signalled the end of the grimmest decade for Irish society (particularly in terms of emigration) for three-quarters of a century.

The late fifties was a time of new beginnings in areas other than the economic sphere. In June 1959 Éamon de Valera offered himself as a candidate for the presidency, and was elected with 538,003 votes, against 417,536 votes for his rival, General Seán Mac Eoin of Fine Gael. On 23 June 1959 he resigned as Taoiseach and was succeeded by Seán Lemass. Two days later he was inaugurated as Uachtarán na hÉireann (President of Ireland).

Remarkably, de Valera was to fulfil two full seven-year terms as President, being re-elected in 1966. Remarkable, in the first instance, because of the man's great age. He was in his ninety-first year when he finally left office as President. More remarkable still, given the fact that since 1952 he had been virtually blind, his presidential years were full of activity, as he scrupulously sought to fulfil the duties of the office. In addition to receiving a host of distinguished visitors, including many heads of state, at Áras an Uachtaráin, de Valera undertook several lengthy and, no doubt, taxing state visits abroad during his fourteen years as President. Perhaps the most memorable and poignant was his visit to the United States of America, the land of his birth, in 1964. During this visit he gave an emotional address to a joint session of both Houses of the Congress of the United States on 28 May 1964. No less memorable and emotional was his address

Éamon de Valera with his mother in America in 1927. His mother re-married and had a new family in America.

Éamon de Valera and his family at his eightieth birthday in 1962. He once said that his greatest personal regret in politics was that political activity had cost him the childhood of his children. He was in prison, on the run or out of the country almost continuously from 1916 to 1924. In later years he was a very attentive grandfather.

to the joint Houses of the Oireachtas in special session in the Mansion House, Dublin, on 21 January 1969 on the fiftieth anniversary of the first meeting of Dáil Éireann.

De Valera completed his second term of office as President on 24 June 1973. Leaving Áras an Uachtaráin he and his wife went to live in retirement at Talbot Lodge, Linden Convalescent Home, Blackrock, Co. Dublin. On 7 January 1975 Sinéad de Valera died, on the eve of the sixty-fifth anniversary of their wedding. Within a few months her husband was to follow. On 29 August 1975 Éamon de Valera died, in his ninety-third year. He was survived by six of his seven children (one, Brian, having been killed in a riding accident) – Vivion, Máirín, Emer, Éamonn, Ruairí and Terry. Éamon de Valera is buried in Glasnevin cemetery, Dublin.

Chapter 2

De Valera and Political Sovereignty: The Idée Fixe

When the young Éamon de Valera returned to Ireland in 1885 the country was on the threshold of a fateful turning-point in its political history. Under the leadership of Charles Stewart Parnell, the Irish Home Rule Party was poised to score a spectacular electoral success in the general election of 1885 – returning 85 members out of 103 in the Irish constituencies, including a bare majority of the members elected for the Ulster constituencies.

Acknowledging the verdict of the Irish electors – and responding to the exigencies of domestic British politics – the great liberal leader, W. E. Gladstone, announced his conversion to the cause of Irish Home Rule. His declared objective was the creation of a "union of hearts," the reconciliation of Irish national ambitions and aspirations with the demands of British imperial interests. Although it produced no immediate change in Ireland's constitutional status, Gladstone's conversion was of momentous importance. A major British party had publicly acknowledged that the Act of Union could, and should, be changed; that a new relationship should be formalised between Ireland and her powerful neighbour; that a new constitutional framework should be established for the governing of Ireland and for the conduct of Anglo-Irish relations. Throughout the whole of de Valera's public life (and indeed continuously since his departure) this central question – the status of Ireland, the extent of her independence, her exact measure of sovereignty (in all its manifold forms, economic, social

and cultural, no less than political) – this central question was to be the governing passion of his political life, the source from which were to spring the bulk of his ideas, aspirations, policies and, indeed, prejudices. Through all the many tortuous arguments, the seemingly jesuitical hair-splitting of constitutional differences, the bitterness and conflict on economic strategy and social policies, which punctuated a long and controversial career in the forefront of Irish public life – this central preoccupation with Irish sovereignty remained the controlling idea, the *idée fixe*, of Éamon de Valera.

What did an independent Ireland, a sovereign Ireland, mean? What should it mean? What form of state should it take? How could it accommodate the sizeable minority (concentrated in the north-east) who did not want to be part of an independent Irish state, but wanted rather to remain in union with Britain? How should an independent Ireland stand in relation to Britain? How should it stand in relation to the international community of states and nations? These were the questions which dominated Irish politics from the time that young de Valera began his schooling in Bruree in 1888, and they were the questions to which he returned again and again right up to his death in 1975.

It was these same questions which confronted the somewhat ascetic-looking young man, already lionised as the sole surviving commandant of the 1916 rebellion, on his release from prison in the early summer of 1917. On 11 July 1917 de Valera was elected for Sinn Féin in a by-election in East Clare. The "new" Sinn Féin, of

n 1916 the insurgents went to prison and internment as villains. A year later heir release was greeted by enthusiastic crowds. Public opinion had switched n a year. The insurgents had played little part in influencing that opinion. Crowds at Westland Row, Dublin awaiting the return of released prisoners.

iamon de Valera was elected a member of parliament for Clare in a by-election n 1917. He was to continue to represent Clare until he became President in 959. Crowds greet de Valera (under the flag) at Ennis Courthouse. His statue ow dominates the Courthouse.

course, was no longer Arthur Griffith's original creation, a minor if lively political movement advocating a dual monarchy on the Austro-Hungarian lines as a formula for the settlement of Anglo-Irish relations, but rather a kind of "popular front" comprising many of the elements (largely republican in sentiment) who had participated in, or who were increasingly coming to endorse in retrospect, the 1916 rebellion. In October 1917 de Valera was unanimously elected President of the reconstructed Sinn Féin, and he himself devised the formula in which the new Sinn Féin announced its objectives:

> Sinn Féin aims at securing the international recognition of Ireland as an independent Irish Republic. Having achieved that status the Irish people may by referendum freely choose their own form of government.

On this platform Sinn Féin swept "nationalist Ireland" in the general election of 1918. In all, Sinn Féin won 73 seats (many of them without a contest), with 26 seats going to the Unionists (overwhelmingly concentrated in Ulster), and a mere 6 seats being retained by the old Irish Parliamentary Party. De Valera was returned for East Clare and for East Mayo, where he routed the Irish Parliamentary Party leader, John Dillon. The elected Sinn Féin deputies who were not in prison assembled in the Mansion House in Dublin in January 1919, constituted themselves Dáil Éireann, and ratified an independent, democratic republic. Immediately, work began to secure international recognition for the newly declared Irish republic, particularly at the Peace Conference in Paris but also in the other world capitals. De Valera was among those deputies who were in prison when the First Dáil met, but having escaped from Lincoln Jail in February 1919 (with the help of Michael Collins, Harry Boland and

Éamon de Valera canvassing for W. T. Cosgrave in Kilkenny at a by-election in 1917. Divisions in the Sinn Féin movement were later to emerge.

others), he was elected Príomh-Aire (later styled President) of Dáil Éireann in early April, and in early June set out for the USA for a major tour to get support (financial, political and diplomatic) for the independent Irish state. He was to remain in the USA until December 1920.

Not even the euphoria and awesome sincerity of the First Dáil, however, could disguise the fact that there were enormous obstacles in the way of the realisation of "the Irish republic" so confidently proclaimed in the Mansion House. Firstly, Britain had no intention of accepting an Irish republic on her flank; and secondly, the strong Unionist enclave in the north-east wanted no part of any Irish state, however modest its claims to

THE WEST'S AWAKE!

MEN OF
NORTH ROSCOMMON,
Ireland Expects You
To STRIKE a BLOW
FOR OUR SMALL NATIONALITY
AND RETURN
COUNT PLUNKETT,

As YOUR REPRESENTATIVE, and FREE HIM from
EXILE, and his Children and your Countrymen from

Prison Chains.

Will **North Roscommon
Loosen** their **Bonds** or act as
Gaolers over **Irishmen.**

The EYES of IRELAND are ON YOU !!

The eyes of your sons and daughters beyond the seas,
and of your countrymen scattered all over the world are
on you.

ALL true LOVERS of IRELAND TRUST NORTH
ROSCOMMON, and WELL THEY MAY,

To Return **COunt Plunkett.**

" Democrat Print," Strokestown

political sovereignty, and certainly had no intention of becoming part of a sovereign Irish republic. The Government of Ireland Act of 1920 effectively allowed the Ulster Unionists to control six counties outside the control or jurisdiction of any state, whatever its constitutional status, which might be set up by "nationalist Ireland." Obviously, nationalist Ireland was not prepared to accept the justice or the permanence of this partition. But for the moment nothing could be done to reverse the development. What was open to question, to struggle and bargain for, was the kind of state which would operate for nationalist Ireland, and it was for this that the war of independence was fought.

De Valera's position at this time – and particularly during his visit to America – was extremely difficult. His public utterances on the subject of Irish independence in the interval between the assembly of the First Dáil and the final split on the Treaty in late 1921 must be related to the audiences he was addressing and to his judgement of the tactical requirements of the moment. He was attempting two distinct – and, in the eyes of many, mutually exclusive – tasks. One was to secure recognition for Ireland's right to self-determination and, more problematically, to gain recognition for the Irish republic as "proclaimed." It was in this context that he publicly opposed Article X of the League of Nations covenant, and played an active part in influencing American opinion against ratifying the League's covenant as originally proposed by President Wilson. Article X enjoined member states "to respect and preserve" the territorial integrity of member states against "external aggression"; and had it been adopted (and agreed to by the USA) in advance of Ireland's right to self-determination being conceded, then, as de Valera argued, it would have

---

he 1918 General Election with a largely new electorate voting for the first time turned 73 seats to Sinn Féin, 26 to the Unionists and only 6 seats for the old ish Parliamentary Party.

copper-fastened Britain's control of Ireland and made the achievement of Irish independence much more difficult. On the other hand, however, de Valera set himself the task of indicating in public a willingness to try to understand, and if possible to allay, legitimate British fears and anxieties about the security aspects of an independent Irish state. This meant striking a hard line on Irish independence (to keep the morale of his supporters from flagging and to conform to his role as Priómh-Aire/ President of the Republic), as well as a conciliatory one, aimed at indicating a willingness to negotiate and to seek terms mutually acceptable to the British and the Irish republicans. It was a difficult tight-rope to walk, as de Valera learned, for example, when he gave an interview to the correspondent of the *Westminster Gazette* in February 1920. In the course of the interview de Valera addressed himself to the problem of reconciling British security needs with Ireland's demand for freedom. He offered what he judged to be helpful suggestions:

> Now I am more than ready to admit that, if the concession of Ireland's right conflicted with the equal right of another nation, that other nation would have a right to object until there had been a proper adjustment between the rival rights.
>
> ... if it were really her independence and her simple right to life as a national state that Britain wanted to safeguard, she could easily make provision for that without in any way infringing upon the equally sacred right of Ireland to its independence and to its life.
>
> The United States, by the Monroe Doctrine, made provision for its security without depriving the Latin republics of the South of their independence and their life. The United States safeguarded itself from the

---

For the first time women over the age of 30 years were entitled to vote in the 1918 election. Extension of the franchise was won because Ireland was part of the United Kingdom. The new electorate promptly voted itself out of the United Kingdom.

sınn ⲣéın

THE WOMEN OF WICKLOW

WILL CAST THEIR

FIRST VOTE

FOR

INDEPENDENCE

VOTE FOR

BARTON

AND A

FREE IRELAND

Patrick Mahon, Printer, Yarnhall Street, Dublin

possible use of the island of Cuba as a base for an attack by a foreign power by stipulating: "That the Government of Cuba shall never enter into treaty or other compact with any foreign power or powers which will impair or tend to impair the independence of Cuba nor in any manner authorise or permit any foreign power or powers to obtain, by colonisation or for military or naval purposes or otherwise, lodgement in or control over any portion of said island."

Why doesn't Britain do thus with Ireland as the United States did with Cuba?

Why doesn't Britain declare a Monroe doctrine for the two neighbouring islands? The people of Ireland, so far from objecting, would co-operate with their whole soul in a regional understanding of that sort.

De Valera made other suggestions also regarding the kind of guarantees which might be given to Britain, citing the Belgian case for example, but it was the Cuban analogy which caused the political storm and showed clearly to de Valera how treacherous indeed was the path to conciliation and accommodation. The fact that the agreement between Cuba and the USA included other terms decidedly less generous to Cuba (i.e. the right of the USA to have military bases in Cuba and to intervene to preserve internal order) gave de Valera's critics plenty to crow about in claiming that he was reneging on Ireland's claim to national independence. In the USA the old Fenian, John Devoy, and the influential judge, Daniel F. Coholan, used the Cuban stick to belabour de Valera, even as he continued to protest that his reference

When Dáil Éireann met for the first time in January 1919 most of its members were either in prison or on the run. The Dáil declared a Republic. As the Volunteers in the War of Independence could not defeat the British forces militarily a compromise became inevitable. The 1919 ratification of the Republic made this difficult.

By April 1919 many more members of the Dáil were able to attend. The front row from left to right is Ginnell, Collins, Brugha, Griffith, de Valera, Plunkett, MacNeill, Cosgrave and Blythe. Soon many of them were to be on the run again.

to Cuba only referred to the specific clause cited. However, neither the abuse of his Irish-American opponents nor the fact that his conciliatory noises were rousing the suspicions of hard-line republican elements in Ireland deflected de Valera from his strategy of publicly taking a moderate stance with a view to opening the door for negotiations with Britain. Back in Ireland in March 1921 he declared:

> Time after time we have indicated that if England can show any right with which Ireland's right as a nation would clash we are willing that these be adjusted by negotiations and treaty.

And the following month de Valera repeated his view that Britain, having recognised Irish independence, could

> issue a warning such as the Monroe doctrine, that she would regard any attempt by any foreign power to obtain a foothold in Ireland as an act of hostility against herself. In case of a common foe Ireland's manpower would then be available for the defence of the two islands.

Nor was it only in the matter of Britain's security worries that de Valera appeared to be (and sought to appear) conciliatory. On the precise *form* of an independent Irish state he became increasingly adept (between 1917 and 1922) at keeping his options open and not playing himself into a corner on the issue of "the republic" *pur et simple*.

Though he continued to assert that for himself the republican ideal remained his guiding ambition, he was careful to indicate publicly a non-doctrinaire position on the precise form of an independent Irish state. As the

Éamon de Valera was to spend most of 1919 and 1920 in the United States seeking recognition for the Irish Republic and financial assistance for the proscribed Dáil. Éamon de Valera with the Rev. Duffy in New York, 1919.

Irish American politics were full of suspicion and division. It was inevitable that de Valera would run foul of some section or another. Here he is with leading Irish-Americans Gough, Cohalan, Devoy, Gavigan and More.

Sinn Féin formula of 1918 had said, it was for the Irish people, free from threat or coercion, to decide on the form of government under which they wished to live. Repeatedly during his tour of America de Valera asserted that self-determination was the objective of the Irish nationalist demands. Again and again he stated: "What I seek in America is that the United States recognise Ireland's case, Ireland's right to national self-determination, that and nothing more." In late March 1921 de Valera wrote: "Our position should be simply that we are insisting on only one right, and that is the right of the people of this country to determine for themselves how they should be governed." By the middle of 1921 he had given ample indications of his willingness to negotiate with a wide range of options still open: " . . . we are thoroughly sane and reasonable people, not a coterie of political doctrinaires, or even party politicians, Republican or other."

These conciliatory noises caused considerable unease among certain elements of the republican forces in Ireland, particularly in the IRA, and de Valera privately had to reassure some of the more active military men such as Ernie O'Malley and Tom Barry that, while the road to negotiation (or, more precisely, the public declaration of an openness to negotiation) was the correct road for the Dáil to take, nevertheless he agreed with the republican militants that Britain's right to rule in Ireland could never be conceded and should be resisted at all times and in whatever manner might seem most appropriate. Not all republicans were reassured in private, however. Many, like Liam Lynch, had "declared for an Irish republic and will not live under any other law," and were deeply suspicious of de Valera's steadfastness. Other republician leaders sounded more intransigent. By August 1920, while de Valera was in America, Michael Collins had briefed newsmen and told them that he would have "no compromise and no negotiations with any British government until Ireland is recognised as an independent republic." This view, shared by many republicans in Ireland, was applauded by important elements of Irish-American opinion, and was contrasted with de Valera's more conciliatory line.

It is important to remind ourselves, therefore, that in certain circles de Valera was perceived as "a trimmer" in the republican camp up to the summer of 1921. Moreover, it was further perceived that he was a mere figurehead, and a rather dispensable one at that, and that the real power-brokers in the Sinn Féin camp were those involved in the military and intelligence side of the war of independence, for example Michael Collins and Dick Mulcahy. It is only fair to say that the military leaders didn't always seek to discourage this view. When the poet W. B. Yeats saw de Valera on a public platform in May 1919 he was disappointed in him, and judged him as follows:

> A living argument rather than a living man. All propaganda, no human life, but not bitter or hysterical or unjust. I judged him persistent, being both patient and energetic, but that he will fail through not having enough human life to judge the human life in others. He will ask too much of everyone and will ask it without charm. He will be pushed aside by others.

More astute political minds than Yeats, working on different assumptions, also concluded that de Valera would be pushed aside. This view penetrated to the British Cabinet. By mid-1921, when his mind was turning firmly to a settlement of the Irish problem, Lloyd George wrote: "The question is whether I can see

Michael Collins. No doubt he is the head and front of the movement. If I could see him, a settlement might be possible."

It was only natural, of course, that those who were, quite literally, calling the shots in the military conduct of the Anglo-Irish war should be considered key figures in any overall settlement. But it is nevertheless important to remember that when eventually negotiations began in July 1921 with de Valera's visit to London for discussions with Lloyd George, the Irish leader was by no means seen universally as the sea-green Robespierre of the Sinn Féin camp.

De Valera rejected Lloyd George's proposal of July 1921, with its opening offer of dominion status for Ireland, subject to certain defence and trade conditions. It is important to understand why these proposals were unacceptable. Firstly, de Valera acknowledged that the dominion status enjoyed, *de facto*, by Canada and Australia, did indeed give them effective control over their own affairs. But this, according to de Valera, was because their immense distance from the imperial centre, plus their historical development, prevented or inhibited Britain from engaging in the kind of interference in their affairs which, under the formula for dominion status, she was legally entitled to. In the case of Ireland, none of these conditions applied. The geographical proximity to Britain, the defence and trade implications of this proximity, and the history of Anglo-Irish relations made it much more likely, if not inevitable, that Britain would be much more energetic in exercising her full prerogatives under the dominion status formula in Ireland than in any of the other distant dominions (for example, under the powers of Governor-General, the Privy Council as the final court of appeal, etc.). In defining the sovereignty of an Irish state nothing could be left to discretion or to informal understanding; rights and conditions must be made explicit.

However, even a substantively strengthened version of dominion status would constitute a real dilution of the republican demand, and could only be considered if the North would come in to an all-Ireland settlement. Otherwise, a 26-county state must be a republic. As de Valera put it during his correspondence with Lloyd George in August 1921:

> A certain treaty of free asociation with the British Commonwealth group, as with a partial league of nations, we would have been ready to recommend, and as a Government to negotiate and take responsibility for, had we an assurance that the entry of the nation as a whole into such association would secure for it the allegiance of the present dissenting minority, to meet whose sentiment alone this step could be contemplated.

These, of course, were the opening rounds of the negotiations, and in the subsequent preparation for the sending of plenipotentiaries to London in October to renew efforts to reach a settlement it is clear that de Valera was already facing the possibility, indeed the likelihood, that substantial compromises would have to be made. The genesis of what came to be known as de Valera's Formula for External Association was already in evidence in the summer of 1921. Despite all the changes of detail which this formula underwent between July 1921 and January 1922, its main features are easy to list. Firstly, Ireland would be completely independent of British control or influence in all its *internal affairs*, but for the purpose of external affairs Ireland would agree to combine with the countries of the British Commonwealth

in an association of free partners, a kind of "partial league of nations". Initially this formula rested on the assumption that Northern Ireland would be part of the new settlement. But gradually this ceased to be the case, and the heart of the matter seemed to be how far would the British be prepared (or forced) to go in respect of the status and sovereignty of the 26-county state? As de Valera was convinced that this would not be far enough to satisfy nationalist aspirations (and, therefore, that the negotiations would break down), he was anxious that the "break" should take place on the partition issue. He did not lead the delegation to the Treaty negotiations, believing that he would be more useful in a fall-back position in Dublin, either as a brake on any precipitate rush into agreement on the part of the delegates or as support for the delegates in the unlikely event of their being able to secure broadly acceptable terms which would still fall short of the demands of the unyielding republican separatists. The five Irish delegates at the Treaty negotiations were Arthur Griffith, a reluctant Michael Collins, Robert Barton, and two men chosen principally for their legal expertise, Éamonn Duggan and Charles Gavan Duffy. The final document to which they put their signatures – the Articles of Agreement – did not satisfy de Valera and a considerable body of nationalist opinion in the Dáil and in the country. The reasons for this division in the Sinn Féin ranks revolve around the central notion of Irish sovereignty, and the way in which the different parties understood it. Neither in terms of territory nor in terms of status did the pro-

Arthur Griffith and Éamon de Valera. Griffith was always seen as the most likely to compromise on the Republic. De Valera probably thought he would be counter-balanced by the hard-line republican Michael Collins.

Arthur Griffith, Éamon de Valera, Larry O'Neill and Michael Collins. De Valera never admitted that he erred in not going to London for the Treaty negotiations. However, after the experience of the Treaty he retained exclusive control of Anglo-Irish affairs in all matters when he became President of the Executive Council and later Taoiseach.

posed Irish state meet republican requirements. On the partition issue, the best that was on offer was a Boundary Commission which, it was rashly claimed, would revise the Border in such a way as to render the revised Unionist area non-viable in economic and political terms, and therefore likely to reach an early accommodation with the nationalists in the rest of the country. But partition was not the decisive question in the Treaty split. Nothing which de Valera or his supporters subsequently proposed by way of an amendment to the terms of the Treaty made any material difference to the *de facto* acceptance of partition pending the intervention of the *deus ex machina*, the Boundary Commission. The real battle was fought on the status of the 26-county state being proposed.

The treaty conferred dominion status on the new Irish Free state; it was to be a member of the British commonwealth of nations enjoying the same rights as the other dominions; common citizenship of the British empire, an oath of allegiance to the king and his successors, and prescribed defence and security obligations constituted the main areas of dispute. As the most bitter moments in the debates centred on the oath of allegiance, it may be helpful to give its precise wording here:

> I ... do solemnly swear true faith and allegiance to the Constitution of the Irish Free State as by law established, and that I will be faithful to H.M. King George V, his heirs and successors by law, in virtue of the common citizenship of Ireland with Great Britain and her adherence to and membership of the group of nations forming the British Commonwealth of Nations.

On the status of the Irish state, the key articles were:

> 1. Ireland shall have the same constitutional status in the Community of Nations known as the British

A meeting of Dáil Éireann in the Mansion House in 1921 to discuss the conditions of the Truce and the pre-conditions of treaty negotiation. De Valera, Griffith and Collins are in front of the Speaker's platform to the left. Behind them are Plunkett, FitzGerald, Cosgrave, O'Higgins and Blythe.

Empire, as the Dominion of Canada, the Commonwealth of Australia, the Dominion of New Zealand, and the Union of South Africa with a Parliament having powers to make laws for the peace, order and government of Ireland and an executive responsible to that Parliament, and shall be styled and known as the Irish Free State.

2.   Subject to the provisions hereinafter set out the position of the Irish Free State in relation to the Imperial Parliament and Government and otherwise shall be that of the Dominion of Canada, and the law, practice and constitutional usage governing the relationship of

the Crown or the representative of the Crown and of the Imperial Parliament to the Dominion of Canada shall govern their relationship to the Irish Free State.

The defence clauses of the treaty stipulated:

6.   Until an arrangement has been made between the British and Irish Governments whereby the Irish Free State undertakes her own coastal defence, the defence by sea of Great Britain and Ireland shall be undertaken by His Majesty's Imperial forces, but this shall not prevent the construction or maintenance by the Government of the Irish Free State of such vessels as are necessary for the protection of the Revenue or the Fisheries. The foregoing provisions of this article shall be reviewed at a Conference of the Representatives of the British and Irish Governments to be held at the expiration of five years from the date hereof with a view to the undertaking by Ireland of a share in her own coastal defence.

7.   The Government of the Irish Free State shall afford to His Majesty's Imperial Forces:

(a)   In time of peace such harbour and other facilities as are indicated in the Annex hereto, or such other facilities as may from time to time be agreed between the British Government and the Government of the Irish Free State; and

Illustration taken from a Gaumont Graphic cinema newsreel of an anti-Treaty meeting in February 1922. The newsreel shows Éamon de Valera addressing a huge crowd in Dublin. By this stage he was no longer President of Dáil Éireann. He was faced with a dilemma. He was opposed to the Treaty. Other, more militant anti-Treaty people were to take up the running and de Valera was soon to be largely powerless to affect the drift towards civil war.

W. T. Cosgrave delivering a graveside oration at the funeral of Kevin O'Higgins in 1927. It was shortly after this that Éamon de Valera was to lead his Party into Dáil Eireann. The experience of five years in opposition in Dáil Eireann helped Fianna Fáil enormously when they came to power in 1932. The men in uniform beside W. T. Cosgrave are ushers in Dáil Eireann.

(b)   In time of war or of strained relations with a Foreign Power such harbour and other facilities as the British Government may require for the purposes of such defence as aforesaid.

It was inevitable, of course, that these terms would be rejected by the hardline republicans, in the Dáil and in the Army (for example, Mellowes, Lynch, O'Connor, Robinson). But they were also too tough for de Valera to swallow. It had been hard enough to bring the likes of Brugha and Stack with him on the broad thrust of External Association; but an oath of allegiance to "a foreign king," full membership of the empire, defence and trade conditions, no real movement on partition, and this to be approved by (on the Irish side) "a meeting summoned for the purpose of the members elected to sit in the House of Commons of Southern Ireland" only: this fell far short of the bottom line of what de Valera, even in his most conciliatory posture, felt to be acceptable.

During the course of the bitterly divisive Treaty debates de Valera was forced to formulate the precise details of his scheme of External Association. This scheme, first presented at the private sessions of the Dáil and subsequently, in amended form, in public session, differed in several crucial respects from the Treaty proposals. Fundamentally, it recognised a different source of ultimate sovereignty for the Irish state. Its very first clause related to

"The Status of Ireland"

1.   That the legislative, executive, and judicial authority of Ireland shall be derived solely from the people of Ireland.

2.   That, for purposes of common concern, Ireland shall be associated with the states of the British

Commonwealth, viz: The Kingdom of Great Britain, the Dominion of Canada, the Commonwealth of Australia, the Dominion of New Zealand, and the Union of South Africa.

4. That the matters of "common concern" shall include Defence, Peace and War, Political Treaties, and all matters now treated as of common concern amongst the States of the British Commonwealth, and that in these matters there shall be between Ireland and the States of the British Commonwealth "such concerted action founded on consultation as the several Governments may determine."

The defence proposals of de Valera envisaged a transitional phase of five years, at the end of which, if a mutually agreed system had not been devised in the interim, the Irish state would become solely responsible for its own defence. The formula on partition was substantially the same as in the Treaty proposals, though Document No. 2 envisaged the terms of an Anglo-Irish Agreement being approved by "a meeting of the members elected for the constituencies in Ireland set forth in the British Government of Ireland Act 1920." Finally, and perhaps most crucially, de Valera's proposals contained no oath of allegiance to the Crown. Instead (in order to be seen to be making some concession to British demands) Document no. 2 proposed

6. That, for the purposes of the Association, Ireland shall recognise His Brittanic Majesty as head of the Association.

De Valera's views, as we know, did not prevail in the Treaty debates. The supporters of the Treaty terms argued that his proposals (which he himself described as "my last effort . . . a poor one. It is only a bad best") had already been rejected by the British; that the British would be prepared to go to war for the difference between the rival set of proposals, but that it was not justifiable for an exhausted Irish people to be asked to resume a war against a powerful army for the sake of the differences between the treaty terms and document No. 2. Furthermore, the main advocates of the Treaty (with few exceptions) claimed, with Collins, that the Treaty offered the "freedom to achieve freedom," a stepping-stone to further instalments of freedom (it is arguable that Collins himself was most intent on securing the evacuation of the British Army, on the completion of which he would have turned to further progress on the political and constitutional front).

De Valera gained little in advocating his Document No. 2 proposal. He failed to carry important sections of the republican camp with him, and his description of the extra concessions he was demanding as "that small difference" or "that little sentimental thing," was hardly likely to win converts from any side of the house. In the event, the Treaty was endorsed by a majority within the Dáil and throughout the 26 counties in a general election, and its conditions were incorporated in the Constitution of the Irish Free State in 1922. The republicans refused to accept the Treaty, and during the civil war de Valera was indeed reduced to the role of figure-head on the republican side, as the militants in the Republican Army (O'Connor, Lynch and others) made all the running, and most of the important decisions. Exhaustion eventually allowed for a revival of political initiative. After the fruitless interval of abstention which followed the civil

Recruits for the new civic guards, 1922. The new state had to quickly establish the means of administering the country. The War of Independence had destroyed the RIC. A new police force had to be established.

Two of the first civic guards in 1922. Uniforms were not yet available, so the gun in the holster became the identifying mark. However, in the future the new civic Guards (Garda Síochána) were to become an unarmed police force.

war, de Valera came to accept the *de facto* existence, authority and operation of the Free State institutions, and by 1926 (at the Sinn Féin Árd-Fheis) he was advocating that in the event of the oath of allegiance being abolished (the only really insuperable obstacle to participating in the political and administrative workings of the state) then "it becomes a question not of principle but of policy whether or not Republican representatives should attend these assemblies." The fiasco of the Boundary Commission in 1925 (where the Commission aborted, and an agreement was made by the Free State government which effectively confirmed the existing "extent of Northern Ireland" and allowed the provision for a Council of Ireland to lapse) gave further ammunition to de Valera's claim that, through the policy of abstention, the republican case was being allowed to go by default and the republican view throughout the country was being effectively disfranchised. If the oath could be set aside, republicans should take their place and democratically fight their corner in the political arena.

The uncompromising republicans were not convinced by de Valera's arguments in 1926, nor indeed at any time thereafter. He failed to carry the 1926 Árd-Fheis with him (by a narrow margin), resigned from Sinn Féin and established his own party, Fianna Fáil, on the 16 May 1926 at the La Scala Theatre, Dublin. The aims of the new party were clearly set out a month previously (17 April 1926):

The Dublin Metropolitan police force had been demoralised and rendered ineffectual by the War of Independence. This group is the last recruitment to the DMP. They finally disappeared as a separate force in the mid 1920's.

Eamon de Valera speaking from the platform in Ennis in 1923. After the end of the civil war de Valera was arrested and spent a year in prison. Upon his release he had to rebuild the defeated anti-Treaty side. By 1926 he had established the Fianna Fáil party. The reins of government were only six years away.

In 1927 elected Fianna Fáil TDs took their places in Dáil Éireann. Here Gerry Boland, Éamon de Valera and P. T. Ruttledge lead Fianna Fáil TDs into Leinster House to sign their names before the Clerk of the House. De Valera maintained that he had taken no oath.

1. Securing the political independence of a united Ireland as a republic.
2. The restoration of the Irish language and the development of a native Irish culture.
3. The development of a social system in which, as far as possible, equal opportunity will be afforded to every Irish citizen to live a noble and useful Christian life.
4. The distribution of the land of Ireland so as to get the greatest number possible of Irish families rooted in the soil of Ireland.
5. The making of Ireland an economic unit, as self-

contained and self-sufficient as possible – with a proper balance between agriculture and the other essential industries.

These were the ultimate aims, and have remained so ever since. But there was, of course, an order of priorities. Addressing the inaugural meeting of the party, de Valera claimed that "a young Irishman's appreciation" of the situation as it then stood would lead him to certain conclusions:

> He would see that by isolating the oath for attack, the whole situation, and England's ultimate control, would be exposed. He could scarcely doubt that, the real feeling of the people being what it is, the oath would fall before a determined assault, and he would set out to attack it as being the most vital and, at the same time, the part most easily destroyed of the entire entrenchments of the foreign enemy. He could see ahead, once the oath was destroyed, promising lines for a further advance, with the nation moving as a whole, cutting the bonds of foreign interference one by one until the full internal sovereignty of the Twenty-Six Counties was established beyond question. Finally, with a united sovereign Twenty-Six Counties the position would be reached in which the solution of the problem of successfully bringing in the North could be confidently undertaken.

This states succinctly the order of business for de Valera and Fianna Fáil, and it was indeed to be the running order for constitutional change when Fianna Fáil eventually came to power in 1932. Before that, however, both de Valera and Fianna Fáil had to take the crucial decision to enter the Dáil, and to take the formal admission oath as prescribed in the Constitution. All efforts to abolish or to set aside this requirement (for example, through the initiation of a constitutional amendment by referendum) had been thwarted by the government. Finally, following the assassination of Kevin O'Higgins (Vice-President of the Executive Council and Minister for Justice and for External Affairs) on 10 July 1927, the government introduced a bill requiring candidates in future Dáil elections to promise in advance to comply with the oath. At this point de Valera and Fianna Fáil decided to enter the Dáil, formally taking the oath simply as an empty formula while denying that it signified any solemn obligation (the removal of the Bible from the table on which the book containing the oath rested was a somewhat theatrical repudiation of the solemnity of the promise of loyalty). De Valera himself left the Clerk of the House in no doubt about his attitude to the whole proceedings:

> I want you to understand that I am not taking any oath nor giving any promise of faithfulness to the King of England or to any power outside the people of Ireland. I am putting my name here merely as a formality to get the permission necessary to enter amongst the other Teachtaí that were elected by the people of Ireland, and I want you to know that no other meaning is to be attached to what I am doing.

Inevitably, whatever de Valera might say, the entry to the Dáil caused much bitter comment, as statements made during the Treaty debates and the civil war were recalled. From different ends of the political spectrum Cumann na nGaedheal supporters and republican abstentionists offered their caustic commentary on de Valera's compliance with the "formality." However, the deed was done. Fianna Fáil were in the Dáil, and would be in power within five years.

Of course, by the time Fianna Fáil eventually came to

COSGRAVE WORKS WHILE DE VALERA SWEARS

VOTE
Cumann na nGaedheal

Issued by Cumann na nGaedheal and Printed by Browne & Nolan, Ltd., Nassau Street, Dublin.

END UNEMPLOYMENT!

VOTE FIANNA FÁIL

Cumann na nGaedheal fought the 1932 election on their record in Government and on the unreliability of Fianna Fáil.

Fianna Fáil fought the 1932 election with offers of better medical, social and economic policies than the Cumann na nGaedheal had provided. With high levels of unemployment and considerable poverty their policies proved more attractive.

power in 1932 the limits of Irish sovereignty had already been progressively advancing for the best part of a decade, through the gradual enlargement of the notion of "dominion status" at successive imperial conferences from 1923 to 1930. These developments (in which the delegates of the Free State had played an energetic part) culminated in the Statute of Westminster of 1931, which effectively confirmed the right of the dominions to control their own affairs without interference from the British government; in effect, as co-equal members of the

Commonwealth. However, despite their active role in the development of imperial policy, the Cosgrave government of the 1920s had become much more defensive of the exact terms of the Treaty, more inclined to treat its provisions as being almost sacrosanct, than had been the case in 1921/2. No doubt the bitterness of the civil war, and the deep scars it left on all aspects of Irish life, offer some explanation for positions on the Constitution of 1922 becoming more entrenched as the decade wore on. Nevertheless it was widely perceived that the Cumann na nGaedhael government was prepared to go to extraordinary lengths (for example, abolishing the right of the people to initiate by petition a referendum on constitutional change) to defend the terms of the Treaty as enshrined in the 1922 Constitution, and particularly the oath of allegiance. Collins's stepping stone seemed in danger of becoming a millstone.

The advent of Fianna Fáil to power in 1932 heralded a period of rapid and dramatic constitutional change. In 1933 the oath of allegiance was abolished (delay being caused by opposition in the Senate). The Governor-General's role and functions were inexorably cut down, prior to the abolition of the office. Other constitutional amendments followed (for example, abolition of appeal to Privy Council). In 1936 the Senate was abolished, and in a move of considerable opportunism de Valera took advantage of the abdication crisis (of Edward VIII) in

The scene outside the Fianna Fáil headquarters in Mount Street in Dublin during the 1932 election campaign. The building is still the Fianna Fáil headquarters. It is now called Áras de Valera.

The Fianna Fáil cabinet of March 1932. Front row from left, Frank Aiken (Defence), P. J. Ruttledge (Land and Fisheries), Éamon de Valera (President of Executive Council and Minister for External Affairs), James Ryan (Agriculture), Tomás Derrig (Education), James Geoghegan (Justice). Back Row, Seán MacEntee (Finance), Seán T. O'Kelly (Vice-President, Minister for Local Government and Public Health), Senator J. Connolly (Posts & Telegraphs), Seán Lemass (Industry & Commerce) and Gerry Boland who was Parliamentary Secretary to the President.

The Blueshirt movement may have had its ridiculous side as with these little girls giving fascist salutes. But given what their European counterparts did when they got into power they cannot be treated simply as a joke.

December 1936 to remove from the Constitution all remaining references to the Crown and to the Crown's representative. This was accompanied by an Act (the External Relations Act) empowering the king recognised by the states of the Commonwealth to act on behalf of the Free State (on the advice of the Free State government) in certain external matters. To a very considerable extent, de Valera had now made a reality of his External Association formula of 1921. But there was more to come.

General Eoin O'Duffy, leader of the Blueshirts, addressing a crowd from the balcony of the Ormonde Hotel, Clonmel in November 1933. The Blueshirts were an early threat to the de Valera government. De Valera's strong response also proved useful to him in his relationship with the IRA.

Blueshirt women marching. Whatever about their ideological views the Blueshirts certainly aped the fascist movements which were spreading throughout Europe.

The new Constitution of 1937, while stopping short of actually proclaiming a republic, gave concrete form to the concept of popular sovereignty in Ireland:

Article 5: Ireland is a sovereign, independent, democratic State.

Article 6,1: All powers of government, legislative, executive and judicial, derive, under God, from the people, whose right it is to designate the rulers of the State and, in final appeal, to decide all question of national policy, according to the requirements of the common good.

Article 6,2: These powers of government are exercisable only by or on the authority of the organs of State established by this Constitution.

With the enactment of the 1937 Constitution and the final removal a year later (as part of the Anglo-Irish Treaty of 1938) of the British naval bases from the 26 counties, the major violations of (and restrictions on) Irish sovereignty, of which de Valera and later Fianna Fáil had complained since 1921, were removed. Even some of de Valera's most implacable critics acknowledged what had been accomplished. The acerbic Seán O'Casey in exile declared that the 1938 agreement had "put a high and well-curled feather in de Valera's cap. His Irish constitution added a pewter button to hold the feather in its place ... " The state may not have been formally pronounced a republic but, as de Valera had

Illustration from the British Movietone newsreel of de Valera speaking from the platform in the January 1933 election. In March 1932 de Valera had to rely on the support of the Labour Party. He called a surprise election in January 1933 and won a clear majority of the seats.

Éamon de Valera with an Irish Independent reporter coming down the steps of Government Buildings. As soon as he was in office de Valera set about changing the articles in the 1922 Treaty he found offensive.

forecast on 23 April 1933, " ... when the time comes, the proclaiming of the Republic may involve no more than a ceremony, the formal confirmation of a status already attained." And so indeed proved to be the case when in 1949 "the dictionary Republic" (as James Dillon had caustically dubbed de Valera's creation in 1945) was formally, and with comparatively little fuss, proclaimed a republic by John A. Costello, Taoiseach of the first inter-party government.

The one major constitutional problem left unsolved by the great changes of the twenties and thirties, the one intractable issue casting its shadow across the 1937 Constitution and across all the other constitutional developments, was partition. Here the reality was that from 1925 onwards, despite all the urgings, the protests and the claims of Dublin, the North had gone its own way, and the constitutional developments of Cumann na nGaedhael and Fianna Fáil alike had left it unmoved. While continuing at every opportunity to assert that partition was unjust, unacceptable and temporary, de Valera, no less than his predecessors, was obliged to come to terms with the awkward fact of the border. The republican state might indeed be merely a "republic manqué" while the country remained divided, but even the 1937 Constitution had to acknowledge reality and to accept that "pending the re-integration of the national territory" the constitutional forms and institutions which sought to establish, in the eyes of the Irish people itself and in the eyes of the international community, the sovereign Irish state, could only have reality and effect within the boundaries of the 26-county state established in 1920/25.

The resolution of many of the most outstanding constitutional problems with Britain, and particularly the removal of the restrictions which the Treaty had imposed, was the key element in de Valera's quest for full political sovereignty for Ireland. But it was not the only element. It wasn't enough that the state should become constitutionally sovereign, it must also be seen to be sovereign. The establishment of an independent voice for Ireland in international affairs was an integral part of the struggle for full Irish sovereignty, and had been so since the First Dáil sent out its diplomatic emissaries, announced itself at the Paris Peace Conference, and generally launched itself in the world of international diplomacy. During de Valera's American tour of 1919/20 he not only invariably placed the Irish problem and Ireland's claims in an international context (for example, making analogies with other "small nations", adverting to the implications of the clauses of the League of Nations Covenant, etc.), but he also gave his views, an Irish view, on other international problems. For example, he was deeply critical in public of the punitive terms being imposed on Germany in the 1919 settlement, and he was among those who correctly forecast that these punitive terms would sow the seeds of future discord. De Valera's identification of foreign affairs as a critical area of government policy is evidenced by the fact that he himself retained the foreign affairs portfolio continuously during his unbroken period as Taoiseach, from 1932 to 1948.

Ireland's participation in the League of Nations (at its sessions in Geneva) seemed to de Valera a particularly fruitful way of proclaiming Ireland's independent voice in world affairs. From 1923 the Irish Free State had played an increasingly effective role among the "small states" at Geneva, and in 1930 had been elected a non-permanent member of the Council of the League. It was de Valera's good fortune that when he went to make his

first appearance at Geneva in September 1932 it was Ireland's turn for the Presidency of the Council, and accordingly de Valera was in the Chair for the opening session of the 13th Assembly of the League. In view of the fact that his activities in America in 1919/20 (and particularly the part he had played in discouraging American affiliation to the League) had not been forgotten, it was scarcely surprising that he should have been received rather frostily at the Assembly. Nevertheless, his unusually lengthy (unusual, that is, for Presidents of the Assembly!) address was full of home truths about problems facing the League, the public perception of its authority and effectiveness, and the relationship between the dictates of the great powers (i.e. those which were militarily strong) and the rights of "small nations" and their need for the collective security which ought to reside in membership of the League. This speech, though received "in stony silence", made a strong impression, and boosted de Valera's and Ireland's stock in international affairs. Nor was it an isolated event. Again and again in the League and elsewhere de Valera stated the principles which he felt should apply in recognising, respecting and protecting the rights of the smaller nations, particularly the right to exercise full political sovereignty. He took a firm stand in the calls for international peace, but was not afraid to take an independent line even on controversial issues. For example, Ireland called for the Japanese withdrawal from Manchuria; supported the entry of the Soviet Union to the League (despite the certainty that this line would be controversial at home); strongly condemned the Italian

Éamon de Valera in London for talks. For most of the 1930s Anglo-Irish relations were strained by the effects of the Economic War. Within a year of that being settled Britain was at war and Éire was neutral.

Douglas Hyde parades at his presidential inauguration in 1938. Éamon de Valera's 1937 Constitution established a President as Head of State and a Taoiseach as Head of Government. The former post was largely titular.

attack on Abyssinia; and resolutely stuck to a non-interventionist position in the Spanish Civil War (despite the emotive sympathy for "Catholic Spain" which existed and which was being worked up in Ireland). In the case of Hitler's Germany, de Valera held that Germany had a just complaint in respect of the Sudetenland (the partitionist bogey clearly influenced his views in these situations), and he was broadly supportive of the policy of "appeasement" (or at least of reaching an accommodation where there were just grounds of complaint) up to Munich 1938. Even as he spared no effort in seeking to find ways of averting war, de Valera was deeply aware of the fragile nature of international relations and, in particular, of the relative powerlessness of the small states, for all their pacific fervour, to prevent war breaking out if the great powers were bent on a trial of arms. As he told the Assembly of the League on 2 July 1936:

> Peace is dependent upon the will of the great states. All the small states can do, if the statesmen of the greater states fail in their duty, is resolutely to determine that they will not become the tools of any great power, and that they will resist with whatever strength that they may possess every attempt to force them into a war against their will.

Three years later this policy moved from the realm of theory into the world of real politics.

Ireland's neutrality in the Second World War is crucial to an understanding of de Valera's version of Irish political sovereignty. Of course all states, if they can manage

Éamon de Valera takes the salute at an army parade at Easter 1941. Neutrality during the war clearly established the reality of Irish sovereignty. But neutral Ireland had few friends and had to defend itself.

During the Emergency the Irish army and the various local defence forces and their auxiliaries quickly grew in numbers. The main problem was equipment and identifying the enemy. Officially it was quite clear that the enemy was whoever invaded Ireland. As the war progressed and co-operation between the British and the Irish armies improved and expanded this became a little less clear.

it, would rather not be involved in war; and, indeed, it was only with great reluctance that some of the great powers became involved. But in the case of Ireland's neutrality there was a special significance in the non-aligned position. It was, in fact, the most unequivocal affirmation that could be made of the full measure of sovereignty which had been achieved by 1939. Given the tortuous route which Irish constitutional developments had followed since 1920, the neutrality position represented a kind of declaration of full independence by the Irish state.

De Valera, it is true, did not make any unequivocal, explicit statement elevating "neutrality" to a level of pure principle. But he did state on more than one occasion the grounds for his position. In a St Patrick's Day broadcast on radio in 1941, he addressed himself to Americans who might be puzzled by Ireland's position:

Some twenty years ago, when, in the cause of Irish freedom, I addressed many public meetings in the United States, I pointed out that the aim of the overwhelming majority of the Irish people of the present generation was to secure for Ireland the status of an independent sovereign state which would be recognised internationally as such and could pursue its own life and develop its own institutions and culture in its own peaceful way outside the hazards of imperial adventure – if possible with its neutrality internationally guaranteed like the neutrality of Switzerland. A small country like ours that had for centuries resisted imperial absorption, and that still wished to preserve its separate national identity, was bound to choose the course of neutrality in this war. No other course could secure the necessary unity of purpose and effort amongst its people, and at a time like this we heed the warning that a house divided against itself shall not stand. The continued existence of partition, that unnatural separation of six of our counties from the rest of Ireland, added in our case a further decisive reason.

On the entry of the USA to the war (in December 1941), de Valera reiterated this view:

The policy of the state remains unchanged. We can only be a friendly neutral. From the moment this war began, there was for this state only one policy possible – neutrality. Our circumstances, our history, the incompleteness of our national freedom through the partition of our country, made any other policy impracticable. Any other policy would have divided our people, and for a divided nation to fling itself into this war would be to commit suicide. Of necessity, we adopt the policy of neutrality.

Ireland's neutrality, once embarked upon, was maintained seriously and with some resolution. Neither deep affection for the land of his birth, nor a genuine appreciation of the part which the USA had played in the emerging Irish state (as a refuge for Irish exiles, and as a source of support for the national movement after 1850), nor yet the acceptance on de Valera's part that in broad ideological terms Ireland clearly belonged to the family of liberal parliamentary democracies – none of these factors, important though they were, inhibited de Valera's firm resistance to such pressure (especially American) as was exerted on the neutrality issue during the Second World War.

Neutrality, however, did not mean total isolationism. In the post-war world Ireland gave clear notice that she intended playing an active and independent role in international affairs. In 1946 Ireland sought membership of the United Nations, but was vetoed (until 1955) by the Soviet Union. However, while declining to enter any military pact (such as NATO, established in 1949), Ireland played an active role in the OEEC and was a founder-member of the Council of Europe. Furthermore, when eventually admitted to membership of the United Nations in 1955, during some of the bleakest years of the "cold war" era (and in the twilight years of de Valera's long innings as Taoiseach), Ireland's voice at the UN on many sensitive issues (such as the admission of communist China, the Suez crisis, the invasion of Hungary) continued to claim its right to sturdy independence in international debates, irrespective of the embarrassment (or worse) which such independence often caused some of Ireland's long-standing friends.

In short, the notion of a sovereign Irish state, deriving its authority from God and the Irish people, unfettered in exercising this sovereignty in domestic and foreign policy, lies at the heart of de Valera's political beliefs and policies. This sovereignty must be jealously guarded. Just as a free Ireland could, without pressure, calmly consider any form of co-operation or free association with Britain, so also in a wider context Ireland as a sovereign state could consider any form of economic or other non-military co-operation with other European states. Co-operation, yes, surrender of sovereignty through integration, no. De Valera was opposed to the idea of a sovereign European parliament, making decisions which an Irish government would have to accept. Ireland was too small to count for much, numerically, in such an assembly. We'd had enough of absorption into a "larger unit" during the period of the Union. Our future lay in protecting our national sovereignty, while remaining open to co-operation with anybody, as it might seem appropriate for us. A classic statement of this position was de Valera's 12 July 1955 speech in Dáil Éireann:

> We have always realised that we are one nation among many and that, as far as physical resources were concerned, our resources were not very great.
>
> We also realised that, small as were our physical resources, there were spiritual ones which were of great value; and we never doubted that our nation, though a small one in the material sense, could play a very important part in international affairs. It was for that reason that, from the very start, back even in 1919 we made it clear that we were willing to co-operate in a real League of Nations ... It was with that view also that we wished to join the United Nations Organisation ...
>
> Isolation, then, or co-operation has to be distinguished as to whether we mean it on the non-military or on the military plane. On the non-military plane there is always possibility of agreement; except, I might point out, that, on the economic side for instance, in the Council of Europe it would have been most unwise for our people to enter into a political federation which would mean that you had a European Parliament deciding the economic circumstances, for example, of our life here. For economic and other reasons we had refused to be satisfied with a representative of, say, one in six, as was our representation in the British Parliament. Our representation in the European Assembly was, I think, something like four out of 120 or some number of that magnitude. That is, instead of being out-voted on matters that we would have regarded as of important interest to us by five or six to one, we would have been out-voted by thirty or

forty to one. We did not strive to get out of that domination of our affairs by outside force, or we did not get out of that position, to get into a worse one. But there again, we were anxious to co-operate to the fullest extent that was consistent with our liberty to look after the fundamental things that were necessary to our continued life as a nation.

One of the things that made me unhappy at Strasbourg was that I saw that, at the first meeting, anyhow, of the assembly, instead of trying to get co-operation and to provide organs for co-operation, there was an attempt to provide a full-blooded political constitution, that there were members there who were actually dividing themselves into socialist parties, and so on, as they might do in a national parliament. As far as we are concerned, whilst we wish well to all those who think that it is in their interest to do that, we certainly felt that we should not be committed as a nation to do it. A nation much more powerful, with her associated states, than we were, was chary of that, and I, for one felt, that we would not be wise as a nation in entering into a full-blooded political federation.

But there are interests which we have in common with other countries. Of course, everybody will admit that peace is one of the outstanding interests and that everything that we can do to foster peace in the world we should do. We have economic interests in common too, and there is no reason in the world why we should not co-operate with any organs that

In 1948 de Valera and Fianna Fáil were put out of office after sixteen years of continuous government. The new government was an alliance of Fine Gael, Labour, Clann na Poblachta, Clann na Talmhan and independents under John A. Costello as Taoiseach. The new cabinet is seen here with the President, Seán T. O'Kelly.

In 1951 Fianna Fáil were returned to power. De Valera relied more or less on his old team. The only new minister was Erskine Childers (back row, right). There were mumblings of discontent in the Fianna Fáil backbenches.

are set up for economic co-operation, provided that that economic co-operation is consistent with our own reasonable well being.

The de Valera years saw the formal powers of sovereignty of the Irish state grow and strengthen: they also saw that sovereignty exercised in international affairs in ways which were, given the size and situation of the state, independent and often courageous. The result was an accretion of political respect, and, indeed, of moral standing for the Irish state in international affairs during the de Valera era. From the 1960s onwards, as new economic strategies and new social priorities carried their political implications into general government, the de Valera legacy came in for considerable revision, as Lemass's vision for the development of Irish society introduced new emphases and new priorities. The transition from de Valera to Lemass had implications for foreign policy no less interesting than the more talked about "new departures" in economic and social policy.

Finally, the price paid for this pursuit of full sovereignty was not inconsiderable. The achievement and exercise of sovereignty by the 26-county state – the relatively rapid progress from dominion status to a republic – tended to widen the gap between the southern state and Northern Ireland. As the southern state progressed to a republic it remorselessly moved farther and farther away from that section of "the sovereign Irish people," Catholics and Protestants, who did not reside within its borders. Indeed, the ideological consensus which allowed for such rapid constitutional change (without serious political convulsion) within the southern state rested on, and was reflective of, other consensual aspects of southern society which also, over time, tended to set it apart from the North. Here, the issue was wider than

the simple one of political independence. What was involved was the *end* for which political sovereignty was
sought. What, for example, were the social and economic
purposes which were to be served by its exercise? In
short, why was there a need for a sovereign Irish state at
all? What kind of Irish society was implicit in the notion
of a sovereign Irish state? These were not mere academic
questions. De Valera, like a long line of Irish nationalist
leaders, had a strong belief in the creative possibilities of
political sovereignty for economic and social development. In fact this idea, that a satisfactory constitutional
status was a prerequisite for (and, for some, even a
guarantor of) Irish economic and social development
and of cultural well-being, had a well-established if rather
complex pedigree in Irish nationalist rhetoric. One of
the central propositions of colonial nationalist rhetoric
in the eighteenth century – from Molyneux through to
the champions of Grattan's "independent" parliament –
was that Ireland's economic prosperity and general well-
being could only be adequately safeguarded by an independent Irish legislature. Nor was it only the colonial
nationalists who had a version (a theory, if one wishes to
so describe it) of political sovereignty, its consequences
and possibilities. One strand of popular Gaelic literature
from the early seventeenth century had repeatedly (if
often unrealistically) predicted a political "liberation" or
revolution in Ireland as a precondition of cultural revolution (by which was meant, in effect, the revival of
Gaelic learning and the restoration to a position of
favour of the Catholic religion). During the period of the
Union these ideas or assumptions about the creative
possibilities of political sovereignty underwent many
subtle changes, but the essential core of belief remained.
Irish economic difficulties during the nineteenth century,

and particularly the catastrophe of the great famine, gave plenty of ammunition to Irish nationalists (of all shades of green) who saw the constitutional status of Ireland as the root cause of all her problems. The body of laws against Catholics had, it is true, been abolished during the nineteenth century, but for many Catholics (including many bishops) there remained a strong historic sense of grievance and a strong conviction that in an independent Irish state the Catholic identity and ethos would be more favoured than they could ever be within the British state.

Even the Gaelic "vision" – in retreat throughout most of the nineteenth century – was revived, albeit in a new form, in the Gaelic League's campaign at the turn of the century. Hyde may have wished his movement to remain apolitical, but for many of his most able lieutenants (as they proved during 1915-16), major cultural and political changes remained inextricably linked.

The post-1917 Sinn Féin leadership was steeped in these assumptions and ideas. Most of those who mattered in the new Sinn Féin (on both sides of the Treaty debate) had been "to school at the Gaelic League." De Valera himself was a representative figure of the new nationalist leadership which emerged under the Sinn Féin umbrella after 1917. He held firm convictions on the creative possibilities of political sovereignty. At the inaugural meeting of Fianna Fáil on 16 May 1926 he was quite explicit on this point:

> I think I am right also in believing that independence – political freedom – is regarded by most of you, as it is regarded by me, simply as a means to a greater end and purpose beyond it. The purpose beyond is the right use of our freedom, and that use must surely include making provision so that every man and

Éamon de Valera with Charles de Gaulle in 1969. Two men often compared, they both believed that they knew intuitively what their people wanted. They shared a suspicion about the development of any European union that would threaten national sovereignty.

woman in the country shall have the opportunity of living the fullest lives that God intended them to live.

De Valera showed skill and energy in moulding the constitutional framework so as to allow for the full exercise of political sovereignty within the 26-county state. The question is, what did he do then with his sovereign state?

Chapter 3

Fractured Sovereignty: Partition

Three articles in the 1937 Constitution represent de Valera's most solemn statement of his attitude towards the North.

Article 2:	The national territory consists of the whole island of Ireland, its islands and the territorial seas.
Article 3:	Pending the reintegration of the national territory, and without prejudice to the right of the parliament and the government established by this constitution to exercise jurisdiction over the whole of that territory, the laws enacted by that parliament shall have the like area and extent of application as the laws of Saorstát Éireann and the like extra-territorial effect.
Article 15, 2.1:	The sole and exclusive power of making laws for the state is hereby vested in the Oireachtas: no other legislative authority has power to make laws for the state.
Article 15, 2.2:	Provision may, however, be made by law for the creation or recognition of subordinate legislatures and for the powers and functions of these legislatures.

De Valera would never subsequently deviate from this position. But it had taken him a circuitous route, starting twenty years before, to reach this formulation.

Just twenty years earlier, following the famous Clare by-election in 1917, de Valera told a meeting that "he did not believe in mincing matters, and would say that if Ulster stood in the way of the attainment of Irish freedom, Ulster should be coerced (cheers). Why should it not? If they did not, he would ask them what would happen to the nationalists under their provisional government if they set up one? Would they coerce the minority? Or, if they did not, and the minority claimed the right to set up a provisional government, that minority would have a minority again of Protestants and Unionists inside of it."

The next year he told a south Armagh audience: "The rock of Ulster unionism must be blasted out of their path."

During his tour of America in 1919 and 1920, de Valera adopted a more restrained attitude. It would have been tactically unwise to have irritated President Wilson with expressions of so forthright a nature, and it would hardly have conduced to impressing American politicians with the sweet reasonableness of the Sinn Féin position. It may be too that his own views were evolving under the impress of the American federal achievement. This must remain hypothetical, however, and in any case his speeches until 1921 belonged to the realm of rhetoric. Sinn Féin's abstentionist policy from Westminster meant that there would be no opposition in parliament to Lloyd George's Government of Ireland Act which imposed partition in 1920. Sinn Féin opted out of that whole debate. Behind its rhetorical smoke screen, Sinn Féin in practice abdicated responsibility for northern Catholics, selling them down the drain in the partition year of 1920. For all practical purposes, it stood idly by. From then on, everything Sinn Féin said or did on partition was a matter of bolting the stable door after the horse had gone.

De Valera found himself having to think responsibly about the North for the first time in 1921, when serious negotiations on Irish independence began with Lloyd George. He had to face then the basic fact that partition was already a reality. A northern parliament already existed. Northern paramilitary forces existed. They could not be conjured out of existence, even by the powerful imagination of Irish nationalists. De Valera was a realist. He concluded that rhetoric must make way for reality. He was not going to risk the chance of independence for the South simply because the North existed. He therefore adopted a strikingly moderate negotiating position, far removed from the belligerence of his early platform performances, in his discussions with Lloyd George following the truce of July 1921. He had to convince Dáil Éireann that compromise was essential and in August 1921 he set out to rivet the Dáil's eyes on reality. He pitched his argument at two levels, the level of principle and the level of expediency. He told the Dáil "it was difficult to have a policy for Ulster when they could not get in contact. Their present aim was to get in touch with them. They had not the power, and some of them had not the inclination, to use force with Ulster. He did not think that policy would be successful. They would be making the same mistake with that section as England had made with Ireland. He would not be responsible for such a policy."

De Valera's solution to the dilemma was county option: "for his part, if the Republic were recognised, he would be in favour of giving each county power to vote itself out of the Republic if it so wished. Otherwise they would be compelled to use force."

De Valera's statement shocked some deputies. But he

refused to budge. He insisted to the Dáil the next day:

> I cannot accept office except on the understanding that
> no road is barred, that we shall be free to consider
> every method. For example, the question of voting
> out of counties or provinces. That would be a way, if
> that came up, a way in which a certain result could be
> obtained. I would be ready to consider that.

De Valera clung to this position for several months.
He opposed the Treaty in December 1921. But that wasn't
because of Article 12, which contained the proposal to
set up a Boundary Commission:

> A commission consisting of three persons, one to be
> appointed by the government of the Irish Free State,
> one to be appointed by the Government of Northern
> Ireland, and one who shall be chairman to be appoin-
> ted by the British government, shall determine in
> accordance with the wishes of the inhabitants, so far
> as may be compatible with economic and geographic
> conditions, the boundaries between Northern Ireland
> and the rest of Ireland.

De Valera opposed the Treaty instead because of the
oath of loyalty to the king of England. In his famous
Document No. 2, his alternative to the Treaty proposals,
he offered no alternative to Article 12 on Ulster. His
proposal in the first draft of Document No. 2 in December
1921 is identical with Article 12 for all practical purposes.
He then had some quick second thoughts. In his revised
draft he made no reference at all to Ulster in the text. He
relegated it to a mere "addendum". This rejected the
right of secession in principle for the six counties, but
hastened to accept it in practice.

Nationalist politicians in the south consistently underestimated northern
Unionists' objections to any form of Home Rule – Bangor, Co. Down displaying
its "Britishness".

The Twelfth of July – an annual opportunity for Unionists to honour their
history.

Resolved: that whilst refusing to admit the right of any part of Ireland to be excluded from the supreme authority of the parliament of Ireland, or that the relations between the parliament of Ireland and any subordinate legislature in Ireland can be a matter for treaty with a government outside Ireland, nevertheless, in sincere regard for internal peace, and in order to make manifest our desire not to bring force or coercion to bear on any substantial part of the province of Ulster, whose inhabitants may now be unwilling to accept the national authority, we are prepared to grant to that portion of Ulster which is defined as Northern Ireland in the British Government of Ireland Act of 1920, privileges and safeguards not less substantial than those provided for in the "Articles of agreement for a Treaty" between Great Britain and Ireland signed in London on December 6, 1921.

This would remain de Valera's basic position for the rest of his life. Nevertheless, he made little reference to Ulster in his speeches in the Treaty debate. He did subsequently claim that he broke with Lloyd George in the truce negotiations in 1921 over the question of partition. He did not. On the contrary, he took every precaution to keep the negotiations going. He went to such lengths to prevent Lloyd George from breaking off negotiations that he had to justify his position to Dáil Éireann in the public session on 17 August 1921 at length.

If it had been demanded of me that, before going to negotiate with the British Prime Minister, I would first of all have to renounce our independent right, I would not have gone. If, on the other hand, seeing the claim that they are putting forward, I had said that, before I went, Britain would have to acknowledge our right absolutely, I might have been held to have been unreasonable because then there would be no question of, or necessity for, negotiations.

In the same way that the people of the North of Ireland can recognise themselves if they want to, we recognise ourselves. Even on such a base there can be negotiations. But if negotiations can only begin when we have given up the right of this country to live its own life in its own way, there can be no negotiations at all with the North of Ireland or anywhere else.

If the North of Ireland – the people of the North of Ireland – are free to regard themselves from their own point of view in going into negotiations with us, they have not to give up that point of view. As far as I am concerned, I would be willing to suggest to the Irish people to give up a good deal in order to have an Ireland that could look to the future without anticipating distracting internal problems. That is what this negotiation has been so far as I am concerned. It has been all the time an attempt to get in touch with the people of the North of Ireland and to tell them that we have no enmity to them, because they are Irish men living in Ireland, and that we were ready to make sacrifices we could never think of making for Britain.

De Valera adopted a conciliatory attitude on the North in 1921. He was also a relative moderate on the question of the Treaty. He opposed the Treaty, but recognised that some compromise with reality was unavoidable, however much he tried to cloak his conciliatory policy in the rhetoric of eternal resistance. He tried to avoid the civil war. He detested the idea of a military dictatorship of the more belligerent anti-Treaty leaders like Rory O'Connor and Liam Mellowes. Once the civil war broke out, however, he found himself dragged along in their wake. There was no further middle ground for him. The militarists distrusted his capacity for conciliation, and relegated him to a relatively minor role during the civil war itself. Only when the militarists were killed could de Valera recover his political influence on the anti-Treaty side.

De Valera was arrested and imprisoned by the W. T. Cosgrave government at the end of the civil war in 1923. When he was released from jail in July 1924 he had to re-establish his credentials with the anti-Treaty forces, many of whom still distrusted him. The problem of partition was now looming larger in the public conscious-ness as it became clear that Northern Ireland was a going concern, and that James Craig, that rock of an Ulster man, had no intention of yielding to either force or blandishments. In the rapidly changing circumstances after 1922 it became politically necessary for de Valera to rewrite history to shift the alleged causes of the civil war from the oath to partition. He was already grasping the possibilities in 1923, and on his release from jail the Ulster card was now the obvious one to play. De Valera got himself arrested in Newry in November 1924, and when the RUC were sufficiently unsporting as to release him he had to have himself arrested all over again in Derry later in the month before achieving the rewarding political investment of a month in a Belfast jail.

The fiasco of the Boundary Commission in 1925 came at an opportune moment for de Valera. It allowed him to adopt a more hardline attitude than he had shown in 1921, and to impose it retrospectively over his past. He would talk no more now about county option. Never-theless, he skilfully used the report of the Boundary Commission to begin detaching the politicians from the

For many Unionists Éamon de Valera represented the greatest threat to their security.

This illustration is taken from a Gaumont Graphic cinema newsreel and purports to show the arrest of Éamon de Valera by the RUC in Newry in 1924. In fact, the "arrest" was staged for the camera.

gunmen in the Sinn Féin party. He argued that if only Sinn Féin had not been pursuing an abstentionist policy from Dáil Éireann it could have defeated the government of Mr Cosgrave over the Boundary Commission. He therefore began using the issue of partition to allow himself to wriggle off the hook of the "oath" on which he had impaled himself since 1921. Partition was so grievous a crime against the nation that it was necessary to enter parliament in order to oppose it effectively. With this sort of argumentation he began to direct the minds of many anti-Treaty TDs and voters to the advantages of abandoning the abstentionist policy.

Unification naturally became the first ultimate aim of Fianna Fáil when de Valera founded the party in 1926. But he had at the same time to reassure the mass of public opinion that he would not embark on a reckless policy to try to conquer the six counties. The Fianna Fáil manifesto for the 1932 election therefore relegated partition to a discreet position in the list of priorities, and immediately followed this up with the further reassurance that:

> We shall strive also to bring British statesmen to realise that the interests of Britain as well as the interests of Ireland are best secured by an understanding and settlement which will permit the people of the two islands to live side by side as independent friendly neighbours – each respecting the rights of the other and co-operating freely in matters of common concern.

De Valera continued to sustain the anti-partition rhetoric once he came into office in 1932. He now became to some extent the prisoner of the successful dismantling of the Treaty. The passage of time was exploding every argument he had advanced for opposing the Treaty, except one. None of his dire predictions came true. The British did not reinvade the Free State. The hated oath could be abolished. He abolished it himself. The governor-general could be abolished. He abolished him himself. The king could be taken out of the Constitution. He took him out of it himself. The Treaty did in fact provide a stepping-stone to full formal sovereignty for the Free State, as Michael Collins predicted it would, and as de Valera denied it could. Partition was the one issue that could not be resolved by unilateral Dublin action. In order to justify the civil war, de Valera therefore had to fall back on the sole issue which continued to loom large in the public consciousness. He had to continue to insist that he had fought the civil war over partition. It became psychologically as well as politically necessary for him to continue to beat the partition drum and to play the Ulster card with ritualistic regularity.

In practice, de Valera did little directly to weaken partition. He refused to establish Fianna Fáil in Ulster, or to permit Ulster nationalist deputies to take their seats in the Dáil. Indirectly, he committed himself to creating a state in the South that could only repel any self-respecting Ulster Protestant. His Constitution of 1937 marked the culmination of this policy.

The Constitution was de Valera's supreme attempt to square the circle of republicanism and Catholicism. He held that it was a constitution for the North as well as for the South, for Protestants as well as for Catholics, for Wolfe Tone and Robert Emmet no less than for Cardinal MacRory and Dr. McQuaid. Nevertheless, once he got Articles 2, 3 and 15 out of the way, de Valera wrote the Constitution as a 26-county constitution. He just forgot about the North. Ulster Protestants may as well not have existed as far as the Constitution was concerned. This wasn't basically a question of Article 44, with its reference to the special position of the Catholic Church.

Article 44, when read in its entirety, simply recognised reality, and was indeed a very moderate official recognition of the influence of the Church in Ireland. In many respects, Article 44 could stand as a liberal, even noble, expression of the principle of religious toleration.

Religion
Article 44.

1.   1 The state acknowledges that the homage of public worship is due to Almighty God. It shall hold His Name in reverence, and shall respect and honour religion.

    2 The State recognises the special position of the Holy Catholic Apostolic and Roman Church as the guardian of the Faith professed by the great majority of the citizens.

    3 The State also recognises the Church of Ireland, the Presbyterian Church in Ireland, the Methodist Church in Ireland, the Religious Society of Friends in Ireland, as well as the Jewish Congregations and the other religious denominations existing in Ireland at the date of the coming into operation of this Constitution.

2.   1 Freedom of conscience and the free profession and practice of religion are, subject to public order and morality, guaranteed to every citizen.

    2 The State guarantees not to endow any religion.

amon de Valera held that his 1937 Constitution was a constitution for the North s well as the South. This view was not shared by people in Belfast.

elfast shipyards. The yard owners feared that if Northern Ireland was not part : the United Kingdom, orders would be lost to the shipyards of England and :otland.

3 The State shall not impose any disabilities or make any discrimination on the ground of religious profession, belief or status.

4 Legislation providing State aid for schools shall not discriminate between schools under the management of different religious denominations, nor be such as to affect prejudicially the right of any child to attend a school receiving public money without attending religious instruction at that school.

5 Every religious denomination shall have the right to manage its own affairs, own, acquire and administer property, movable and immovable, and maintain institutions for religious or charitable purposes.

6 The property of any religious denomination or any educational institution shall not be diverted save for necessary works of public utility and on payment of compensation.

Article 44 did not create insuperable barriers to conciliation with the North, insofar as religion was a major cause of division. It was rather that the whole constitution was suffused by the prevailing ethos of Catholic doctrine, particularly in the clauses which subordinated Protestant to Catholic consciences. The Constitution did guarantee equal rights before the law. But that law was powerfully tinged by Catholic influences. And Protestant parents had no rights against Catholic principles. That de Valera could assume that the Protestant people of the North would permit such a violation of their family rights, as they conceived them, baffles belief. If they were that supine, they would long before have bowed the knee.

De Valera made no provision for a revision of the Constitution in the event of unification. The Constitution contained no clause anticipating, as in the West German Basic Law of 1949, for instance, that it would cease to have validity when unification was achieved, and that a new constitution would have to be approved by the majority of the whole people. He told the Fianna Fáil Árd-Fheis in 1937: "As far as I am concerned, on the basis of that constitution the next move forward must be to get within that constitution the whole of the thirty-two counties of Ireland."

The Constitution, perhaps inevitably, became the plaything of party politics even before it was enacted. A general election was due before January 1938. Fianna Fáil's prospects no longer seemed as promising as they

To Unionists the South was a Catholic state. The identification of Church and State was brought a stage further by the 1932 Eucharistic Congress. This altar was on O'Connell Bridge.

had been in 1933. De Valera hit on the happy thought of holding a general election and a referendum on the Constitution on the same day, in the hope that the voters who supported the Constitution would also vote for Fianna Fáil. He linked the Constitution closely in the public mind not only with Fianna Fáil but also with the Church. To ensure popular support for the Constitution it was essential that the Church should not oppose it. De Valera had to include clauses that would satisfy the Church, and which also incidentally probably happened to coincide with his personal views. He therefore brushed aside Frank MacDermott's motion in the Senate to postpone the introduction of the Constitution: "Since, while purporting to establish a constitution for the whole of Ireland, it offers no basis for union with the North and contains various provisions tending to prolong partition."

Back in 1921, in the course of the Treaty debate, de Valera had courageously argued: "This is an Irish treaty. Everybody, North and South, has a right to be present at any decision which has reference to the Irish nation." Now, sixteen years later, his Constitution of 1937 also purported to be an Irish constitution. But everybody did not have a right to be present. De Valera revealed the partitionist mentality in a flash when he told the Fianna Fáil Árd-Fheis that the Constitution had been passed by "a majority of the Irish people". It had not been passed by "a majority of the Irish people". It had been passed by a narrow majority in the south, and by nobody in the North. "The Irish people" stopped at the border.

The Constitution was therefore a partitionist constitution, despite de Valera's passionate protestations to the contrary. It was designed for the 26 counties. It ignored the way of life of Ulster Protestants over whom it claimed sovereignty.

The Constitution came as a party political gift to the ailing Prime Minister of Northern Ireland, James Craig, now Lord Craigavon. Ulster was suffering from the worst slump in her history. His own leadership of the Unionist party was weakening before the threat posed by the rise of so-called Progressive Unionism, which demanded more attention to social and economic problems. Craigavon was desperate for an issue that would divert attention from internal difficulties and failures. He pounced on de Valera's Constitution to rivet Ulster Protestant eyes on the primacy of the border issue, and to divert internal discontent to the foreign southern devils once more. The moment de Valera's Constitution came into effect Craigavon called a snap election and swept the boards, crushing all internal Unionist opposition.

De Valera, for his part, pulled off a skilful negotiating feat with Britain in concluding the Anglo-Irish Agreement in the spring of 1938, which returned the ports occupied by the British navy to Ireland. Ironically, de Valera's achievement in winning back the ports allowed Craigavon to trump de Valera's ace once more. The Ulster ports were not crucial to British sea defences of the Atlantic supply routes as long as Britain held the southern Irish ports. But once she abandoned the southern ports, then the Ulster ports became vital for her very survival. The convoys bringing the crucial supplies from America had to come around the North of Ireland once the southern ports were no longer available. Only then could they be protected by air and sea cover from Ulster. Craigavon could laugh up his sleeve at de Valera's negotiating triumph on the ports. For this

triumph deprived de Valera of a serious bargaining hand for Ulster co-operation during the Second World War. It handed Craigavon a lethal weapon in his struggle against de Valera's irredentism. It copper-fastened the veto power of Ulster Protestants over any Anglo-Irish attempt at solving partition. It is not clear whether de Valera appreciated the implications for partition of his success on the ports in 1938, although it would be surprising if so shrewd a political mind hadn't grasped the consequences. Neither is it clear whether northern nationalists appreciated those implications.

Another of de Valera's apparent triumphs, his persuading the British not to impose conscription on Northern Ireland during the war, emphasised even further the crucial importance of Ulster Unionists to British security. It made Britain even more dependent on Ulster "loyalists," reminded her how fortunate she was to be able to rely on them in the face of Catholic hostility or indifference, and riveted partition even more firmly on the country.

The Second World War brought several further ironies on the unity issue. De Valera told the Fianna Fáil Árd-Fheis in 1937: "Without the unity of Ireland you cannot have independence of Ireland and everybody knows it." The Second World War proved that one could. Neutrality was the ultimate badge of independence. So possible was it to have independence without unity that de Valera in 1940 dismissed Churchill's suggestion that Ireland should enter the war in return for a British declaration in

When Fianna Fáil first came to power it was sometimes difficult, especially at grassroots level, to differentiate between the party and the IRA. With the responsibility of government, however, that differentiation became progressively clearer. Here, in an illustration taken from a British Paramount cinema newsreel, Maurice Twomey, the chief of staff, delivers a graveside commemoration address to the IRA.

Éamon de Valera made few trips into Northern Ireland. In earlier times the Northern authorities imposed an exclusion order. Later he had little reason to travel. De Valera talking to a RUC Divisional Inspector in 1952.

favour of a united Ireland, on the grounds that a British declaration "gives no guarantee that in the end we would have a united Ireland".

While de Valera rightly resisted pressure from Britain and the USA to enter the war, he made sure that in practice Ireland would be neutral for Britain. The Irish and British military authorities planned co-operation in the event of a German invasion. De Valera maintained an important supply of labour and of food to Britain during the war, which the British considered sufficiently important for them in turn to provide badly needed shipping space and insurance facilities for imports to Ireland. The extent of Irish support for the British war effort was happily concealed, as far as de Valera was concerned, by Churchill's ungracious comments at the end of the war. These gave de Valera an opportunity, which he seized with his superb instinct for the political jugular, to make a dignified reply, in which he used partition as the justification for neutrality. Some of the argument was logically juvenile, but that bothered few in Ireland. The style counted for more than the substance.

It was ironic that de Valera should have reasserted himself as the defender of the Irish claim to unity at the end of the war, for the war not only drove North and South even farther apart than before, but also drove a wedge between de Valera and the IRA. The alliance of conviction in the 1920s had become an alliance of convenience in the 1930s. After about 1936 it ceased to be an alliance in any meaningful sense, though there remained a wary mutual respect, and continuing personal contacts. When the IRA began a bombing campaign in England in January 1939, de Valera denounced them. When the Second World War broke out de Valera appointed Gerald Boland Minister for Justice. Boland was a no-nonsense hard man. He did not shirk tough decisions. He quickly interned seventy IRA suspects. When IRA men went on hunger strike in Dublin in 1939 de Valera initially temporised. He released Patrick McGrath, who appeared to be dying, after twenty-three days on hunger strike. But in April 1940 he refused to release two more prisoners on hunger strike, Darcy and McNeela. They died. When McGrath was convicted of the murder of a detective in August 1940, de Valera remained deaf to the familiar appeals. Several IRA men were executed during the war for murdering policemen and other crimes. De Valera defied the usual pressures that arise in these circumstances.

After the war de Valera referred less frequently to the North, except for ritualistic purposes. He did a world tour after losing the election of 1948 to expose the injustice of partition. This was a response to the attempt by the first inter-party government, and in particular by Séan MacBride, the leader of Clann na Poblachta and Minister for External Affairs, to supersede de Valera as the custodian of republican virtue. To prevent MacBride stealing his thunder on partition, de Valera struck a high publicity pose. He found the world sufficiently absent-minded to have other problems on its conscience after the Second World War. But that didn't really matter. The tour was essentially an Irish election tour, not a world tour except in a purely geographical sense. When de Valera returned to office between 1951 and 1954 he actually toned down the strident anti-partitionism of MacBride. Ironically enough, after de Valera lost the election of 1954 it was MacBride who helped to bring him back to office in 1957. When the IRA border campaign began in the winter of 1956 MacBride withdrew his support from the inter-party government of John A. Costello, and precipitated a general election in 1957, partly because of Costello's lack

A simple assertion outside the Unionist Party headquarters in 1954.

of sympathy for the IRA. The election returned de Valera with a massive majority. Far from adopting MacBride's attitude, however, de Valera moved decisively to crush the IRA. He reintroduced internment in the Curragh and left no doubt about his determination to assert the authority of his government. When de Valera finally resigned as Taoiseach in 1959, there were still many IRA men in the Curragh.

During his life de Valera used a variety of arguments to justify his attitude towards the North. He insisted in 1925 that no section of the nation, as he called it, had the right to opt out of the nation:

All sections and classes within the nation, whatever their political opinions, are entitled to equal rights as citizens and fair play; but no section, north or south, east or west, is entitled to secede from this nation, and secession ought not to be tolerated and, if it can be prevented, ought to be prevented, and on no account whatever should the national consent be given to it.

Ulster Protestants of course denied they belonged to the nation in the first place. They could not therefore secede from a nation to which they did not belong. De Valera replied they had no right to self-determination because they lived on an island. It was not only history, but geography, that defined the Irish nation, and behind geography stood God. God made Ireland an island. And God reputedly intended islands to be, by definition, nations. In 1939 de Valera contended:

I think that the whole of this island is the national territory. I know that people sitting down calmly and thinking of the history of nations and national territories would tell me that national territories change from time to time; that there have been changes in the boundaries of states, in national boundaries in Europe, over the course of centuries; and that in the case of Ireland too, if that happened, well, something had happened which was not unique. There is a certain amount of truth, we must admit, in that contention; but, as was said by Signor Mussolini in a famous letter which he wrote, I think it was last September or October, that there is something about the boundaries that seem to be drawn by the hand of the Almighty which is very different from the boundaries that are drawn by ink upon a map: frontiers traced with ink on other ink can be modified. It is quite another thing when the frontiers were traced by Providence. It is vain and foolish, of course, to try to prophesy or to look into the future, but I do not think that any generation of Irish men living in this island will ever be satisfied – those of them at any rate, who regard themselves as having a connection with the historic Irish nation – as long as a single square inch of the island was outside the control of the nation.

In logic, this amounted to saying that if there was one person who regarded himself as having a connection with "the historic Irish nation" then he had a right to the dictatorial control not only over Ulster Protestants but over every other inhabitant if only he could enforce it, at least as long as Ireland remained an island. "The historic nation" combined with God and geography to deny to the mere living people any right to self-determination.

De Valera's second contention was more prosaic. Accepting – for argument's sake – the Ulster Protestant position that they constituted a local majority, he replied – irrefutably – that by that very criterion, they had no right to claim areas with local Catholic majorities, including south Down, south Armagh, Fermanagh, Tyrone, and west Derry.

De Valera's objectives were clear enough. The dilemma arose over the methods and tactics to be employed. He never rejected the moral right of the South to coerce the North. The first ultimate aim of Fianna Fáil, reunification, was to be achieved by using "At every moment such means as are rightfully available". He assured Fianna Fáil in his inaugural address in May 1926 that "We shall at all times be morally free to use any means that God gives us to reunite the country and win back the part of our Ulster province that has been taken away from us." In the atmosphere of the 1920s his listeners would have saved God the trouble of deciding the morality of means. "Any means that God gives us" can only have meant force to most of his audience. He was more explicit when he told the Irish Senate in February 1939:

> I am not a pacifist by any means. I would, if I could see a way of doing it effectively, rescue the people of Tyrone and Fermanagh, south Down, south Armagh and Derry city from the coercion which they are suffering at the present time, because I believe that, if there is to be no coercion, that ought to apply all round. If we had behind us the strength of some of the continental powers – I can say publicly what I have said privately – I would be perfectly justified in using force to prevent the coercion of the people of south Down, south Armagh, Tyrone, Fermanagh and Derry city. Would I go further than that? Remember, I do not think I would have solved the question of partition simply by relieving them from coercion. Even though I would feel justified in doing it, and probably would do it, still I cannot blind myself and could not blind myself to the fact that the problem of the partition of this country would remain, because a portion of it would still be cut off.

Nor did de Valera renounce in private the right to use force that he claimed in public. His Senate speech was no mere rhetorical exercise. He told Neville Chamberlain and other British Cabinet negotiators in 1938 that "In his view, the coercion of Northern Ireland would, in all circumstances, be justifiable."

Nevertheless, after his first heady invocation of force as the solution to the Ulster question in 1917 and 1918, de Valera never subsequently proposed an actual policy of conquest in practice, as distinct from justifying it in principle. Why then did he reject the use of force in practice, while refusing to condemn it in principle? His answer was simple. The price for Ireland of unification by force would be too high – higher even than the price of partition, however loathsome. After telling Chamberlain in January 1938 that force would be justifiable he went on to say that "he would not himself favour a policy of coercion as he was certain that this would merely create greater difficulties than it would solve."

It may be that his reflections on the legacy of brooding bitterness left by the civil war in the South led him to the view that the price of unity would be intolerable if it was to result in a comparable legacy after unification. He told the Fianna Fáil Árd-Fheis in 1937:

Force ... was not one of the methods to be used for the removal of partition. Force would defeat itself, and they would not get that basis of co-operation between all the people which was most essential if there was to be national unity.

He repeated the same message in 1939:

I don't believe that force is the solution, though I don't say that force, if it did hold out prospects of success, should be eliminated. I see it getting this country into a perpetual mess ... The application of force would not get us what we ultimately want. We want a contented community. We do not want to have a new source of war here.

Nearly twenty years later, when the new IRA border campaign provoked him into re-introducing internment, he told another Árd-Fheis in 1957: "If we brought in by force the part of the six counties that was opposed to us, we would have left an abiding sore that would have ruined our national life for generations." Even if force was militarily successful, he seemed to be saying, it would still remain politically unsuccessful. At that same Árd-Fheis in 1957, immediately after five IRA men were blown up by a land mine near the border in Louth, he warned his party bluntly:

> In this organisation if you want to play your part, you cannot be in both camps. You either believe in the policy of this organisation or you don't. I ask you very sincerely, if you want to avert tragedies like those we have had recently and if you want to avert far greater tragedies and save these young people from themselves, not to encourage them by foolish talk.

De Valera then rejected the use of force in practice after 1921. Nevertheless, the rejection remained on grounds of tactics, not of principle. Why then did he adopt so stern an attitude towards the IRA in the Second World War and again after 1957? Should a mere difference of emphasis concerning tactics justify execution? Were the IRA not his own legitimate successors – or at least the legitimate successors of his civil war persona? De Valera replied to the taunt that he was now killing men who were simply pursuing his own policy of twenty or thirty years before, with the reply that circumstances were now quite different. He claimed the Irish people had no chance to pronounce a free verdict on the Treaty. They were morally coerced into supporting it. But they had pronounced a free verdict on the Constitution in 1937. There was now a legitimate government in Ireland. Disloyalty was treason. Only that government had the moral authority to use force. If force were to be used against the North, if a new civil war was to be launched, it could only be done with the authority of the Dáil. Twenty years later he repeated that argument even more emphatically:

> There is no authority for the use of force outside the authority that is derived from this house. There can

This illustration is taken from a Pathé cinema newsreel, and shows an Armistice Day celebration in Longford in 1925. Many more Irishmen died fighting in the Great War than in the War of Independence and the Civil War combined. Yet by the late 1920s their sacrifices were commemorated less and less.

be but one government and one army in this country if it is going to last. We as a responsible government have got to do everything in our power to see that fact is realised. We do want support – the support of public opinion – and remember, those who might have any secret sympathies with those young men are doing a bad day's work for them if they encourage them in any way. If these young men are brought up against the State, the full authority and power of the State will have to be used in order to vindicate the authority of the State.

116

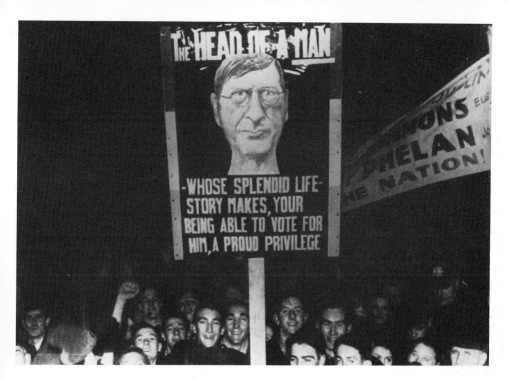

THE HEAD OF A MAN

-WHOSE SPLENDID LIFE-
STORY MAKES, YOUR
BEING ABLE TO VOTE FOR
HIM, A PROUD PRIVILEGE

An election placard for Éamon de Valera, 1948. Despite the sentiments expressed, de Valera was out of office after sixteen years continuous rule. One of the parties that contributed to his defeat was Clann na Poblachta who took republican votes from Fianna Fáil.

But de Valera had given many a hostage to polemical fortune in his earlier career. An IRA man might reply that if majorities had no right to do wrong, as de Valera had pronounced in one of his own most haunting phrases in 1922, it didn't matter what the Dáil decided. The majority, in the Dáil or outside it, had no rights against the sacred egoism of the "historic nation". De Valera was now turning the argument used by the pro-Treaty side against himself in 1922 against the IRA. He could not admit this. Therefore he had to rewrite the history of the civil war in order to preserve the sense of historical continuity in his position and to vindicate his later attitude. He told the Fianna Fáil Árd-Fheis in 1957:

> There has been a wrong interpretation put on our history over the past forty years. They tell you that we who were in the republican army were acting as they are acting. This is not true .... They talk about the civil war and say, "Oh, yes, you went into a civil war and you didn't care about the people's will". I say we did .... We fought to maintain the Republic that was set up by the Irish people, that the representatives of the Irish people were sent to Dáil Éireann to uphold, the Republic that they swore to uphold.
>
> Our position was that the representatives were elected to maintain the Republic and that they had no right to turn down the Republic without the people's will .... They said we wanted civil war. We did not; we did everything in our power to prevent it. The new Dáil was to meet within two days after the time in which the Four Courts were attacked. It wasn't we who forced the civil war. It was they who didn't allow Dáil Éireann to meet.
>
> If we are going to have Irish history of the last forty years put up as excuses, let us have true history .... The people whose names are being called down would have spurned the idea these people have today of being able to act on their own initiative.

This may indeed have been partly true of de Valera himself, who had pursued his own Via Dolorosa between the Treaty and the civil war, desperately clutching for compromise. It was most certainly not true of Rory O'Connor. He openly admitted he was willing to impose the military dictatorship against the popular will if necessary.

De Valera's interpretation of the events of 1922 must

have sounded highly fanciful to his critics, whether of pro-Treaty or IRA vintage. De Valera's tortuous attempt to align the rights of the "historic nation" with the rights of "the people" patently failed to impress the militaristic minds. Once he himself had invoked the "historic nation" against the people, he left himself with no logical reply to those who chose to appoint themselves guardians of the eternal rights of the "historic nation" against the mere transient majority of the people.

There can be no doubting de Valera's genuine conviction that a solution imposed on the North by force would be worse than no solution at all, because it would leave generations of bitterness behind. But why should this be so? His prophecy suggested that he felt the roots of Protestant difference must lie very deep indeed. It is therefore surprising to find that he offered no sustained analysis of the nature of Ulster Protestant demands for self-determination. He denied that the differences between unionist and nationalist owed their origins to racial, or to religious, or to economic factors. His only explanation was that they were due to English party politics, with English Tories mesmerising Ulster Protestants into believing they were different from Irish Catholics. He told the *Evening Standard* in a famous press interview in October 1938:

> It would be completely misleading to consider the present Irish divisions as racial .... The existing partition is based fundamentally on party political differences. Party politics in Britain originated it, and similar politics keep it alive today. Certain factors give partition a religious complexion, but the division is not based on religion.

If de Valera felt, however, that differences could be attributed to so superficial a reason as English party politics, why then should not reconciliation occur quickly once the link with Britain was broken, and English party politics could no longer stoke the fires of hatred? De Valera's anticipation of generations of smouldering resentment seems exaggerated in the light of his analysis of the origins of the conflict. It is only if his analysis is wrong, and the conflict drew its inspiration from deep, instinctive, and indigenous racial and religious hatreds that de Valera's prophecy can carry conviction. If his analysis is right, his predictions are unconvincing. If his predictions are convincing, his analysis is suspect.

After the twists and turns of the period 1917-22, de Valera's policy on the North remained reasonably consistent for the rest of his life. Ulster Protestants should be persuaded, but not coerced, to join a united, federal Ireland. He made clear time and again that he felt a federal solution to be the most sensible. In his *Evening Standard* interview in 1938 he said:

> I'd say to the rulers of Northern Ireland: "Keep your local parliament with its local powers if you wish. The government of Eire asks for only two things of you. There must be adequate safeguards that the ordinary rights of the nationalist minority in your area shall not be denied them, as at present, and that the powers at present reserved to the English parliament shall be transferred to the all Ireland parliament. I assume there would be no opposition on the part of Great Britain to such a solution if you accept it."

His 1937 Constitution appeared to keep the door open for such a solution. Article 15.2 specified that the Oireachtas could make provision "for the creation or recognition of subordinate legislatures and for the powers and functions of these legislatures". As Stormont was the only subordinate legislature which could be "recognised", this article presumably provided de Valera's tactical solution to partition. It does not of course tackle the further problem of whether the 1937 Constitution would then have to be implemented in Northern Ireland. And that problem would surely have to be tackled if Ulster Protestants were to be tempted to agree in the first place to a federal solution.

De Valera rejected force. What alternative did he offer? At one stage he seemed to hope that the solution lay with the British. He argued in 1938 that Britain had only to put pressure on her friends in Northern Ireland to "convert" them to the realisation that a united Ireland was in Britain's own best interests. Nevertheless, he showed that he himself didn't believe this when he rejected British attempts in 1940 to persuade him to enter the war as a quid pro quo for a British commitment to the idea of a united Ireland. He very sensibly replied that Britain could not guarantee to deliver the goods. But this cut the ground from under his own argument that all Britain had to do was to persuade Ulster Protestants to enter a united Ireland. Nevertheless, de Valera's conviction that unification was not only in Ireland's but in Britain's best interest was quite genuine. He returned to the point time and again throughout his life. He didn't hesitate to argue during the impassioned Treaty debates that "One of my earliest dreams, next to securing Irish independence, was that there might be reconciliation between the people of these two islands." In his victory address following Fianna Fáil's triumph in the general election of 1932 he reiterated:

> My desire has always been to bring about the friendliest relations between Britain and Ireland ....

But partition precluded real friendship. He pushed hard if hopelessly in the period before the Second World War to trade off the prospect of Irish co-operation for a British initiative on partition. A united, independent Ireland, he told the *Evening Standard* in 1938, "would be the most solid of all reasons for Ireland's deciding to keep afloat with England". When he heard of the German attack on the Low Countries in 1940 he responded:

> My one regret in a time like the present is that there is still a cause of difference between the two countries. I believe, in trying to look into the future, that the destiny of the peoples of these two islands off the coast of Europe will be similar in many respects.

In private he proclaimed himself to Malcolm MacDonald an almost passionate Anglophile in 1937. He portrayed himself as a prisoner of his past, who could take only faltering steps towards permanent reconciliation with Britain.

> Ireland's freedom was bound up with the freedom of Great Britain; if the latter were threatened the former was also threatened .... There was a time when he was in favour of Ireland breaking her connection with the empire. But that time had gone by. Later, he had been in favour of the Irish declaring a republic, and so breaking with the empire, but afterwards coming back into association with it. He had thought that process necessary in order to establish Ireland's independence.

But the declaration of the Imperial Conference of 1926 and the Statute of Westminster, under which the dominions were recognised as equal in status with Britain,

> had brought changes in the situation. He no longer thought it necessary for Ireland to break away from the Commonwealth in order to establish her freedom.

After the war de Valera supported the policy of neutrality because of partition. But he phrased himself in so elliptical a manner that it seems possible he would have actively considered the possibility of membership of NATO in the event of unification:

> If we were not distracted with the problem of partition, it might be very easy for a government to prepare a line of national defence policy. Even though it might not get agreement from everybody, they would be able to put forward a definite line of national policy which they, as representing the majority here, would put through. I can understand that, if we had not this problem of partition, which is a paralysing problem under present circumstances, paralysing practically for everybody who is thinking in terms of national defence, then it is quite possible that, although there might be a division of opinion in this house, a policy could be put forward by which this country would take the line of action which is taken by other small countries, of combining with other people for defence. But that is out of the question for us now.

If neither force, nor British influence, could end partition, what alternative did de Valera have left? The answer was none. He told the Dáil in 1951:

> I have not taken the view that we will force it by military action, forcing the people in the North to come in, or that we were likely to cajole them either. . . . . I do not want to pretend that the solution is around the corner, but I do say that we will proceed with the same tenacity of purpose in that regard as we have with regard to many other things. I do hope that we will be favoured with good fortune.

In other words, de Valera had no answer. He conceded this rather sadly in his 1957 Árd-Fheis address. Echoing his words to the Dáil in 1921, he told Fianna Fáil:

He would welcome a round table conference with the leaders of the British and Six County governments, and not only a three corner conference but a bi-lateral conference between ourselves and the people of the Six Counties; but he could not bring such a conference about. If you are asking people to a conference, they must be willing to come.

This then was the legacy de Valera left to his successor, Seán Lemass, in 1959. Lemass pursued a policy that showed distinct elements of both continuity and change compared with de Valera's. He continued de Valera's rejection of force, and largely on the same grounds. He took the view that a southern conquest of the North would poison Irish life. If the South conquered Ulster he felt it would be obliged to set up a police state, which would corrode democratic politics in the South no less than in the North.

Lemass, however, was by nature an optimist and an activist, where de Valera tended increasingly as he grew older towards a brooding fatalism, which pushed the achievement of the "ultimate" aims of Fianna Fáil ever further into the future. De Valera might denounce the IRA, but he would make no attempt to create a southern society that might attract Ulster Unionists, or indeed anybody else, to join it. Back in 1933 he did tell the Fianna Fáil Árd Fheis that the way to unity would be through the creation of a southern society that unionists could be proud to join. But few northern Protestants could be codded into believing twenty-five years later that such a society had emerged, or would emerge, in the South. De Valera proclaimed in 1958 that Ireland's sun was only rising. It seemed a very faint sun indeed to hundreds of thousands of Irish men and women who had fled the country since 1945. The gap in living standards between North and South widened sharply after 1939. The northern economy boomed during the war while the southern economy stagnated. The gap widened further after the war when Stormont went along, however reluctantly, with the welfare state created by the Labour government in Britain. While the South staggered from one economic crisis to another, the North enjoyed unprecedented prosperity. She had almost full employment, far more generous welfare payments, far better educational opportunities than the South, even for Catholics. The welfare state in the North placed higher value on the family, and on motherhood, than did the Catholic South. De Valera wrote motherhood into the Constitution. But fewer mothers died in childbirth in the North, and fewer children died in infancy. The problems of mothers and children in the South roused only occasional recognition beyond the realm of rhetoric, as Dr Noel Browne was to discover with his Mother and Child Scheme in 1951. The manner in which the Catholic hierarchy appeared to intervene on that occasion came as a God-send to Ulster unionists, who were able to claim that it obviously justified everything they had said about Home Rule being Rome Rule.

De Valera refrained throughout his life from explaining how he expected anybody actually to want to join a state from which a quarter of its own people had fled since independence. And emigration was rising, not falling, during the futile 1950s. How a state that was patently failing to satisfy the expectations of thousands of Catholics who were flying from it should somehow simultaneously attract into its withering embrace Protestants who felt themselves born free outside it, took some explaining. It got none.

While most of his arguments echoed those of de Valera,

Lemass believed that words were not enough. He hoped to open a window towards the North in two directions. Firstly, he felt that by improving the quality of life in the South, by creating a southern state that was no longer making economic refugees out of thousands of its citizens every year, he could offer a more attractive alternative to his northern countrymen. By establishing closer economic relations with the North, symbolised by his meetings with Captain Terence O'Neill in 1965, he hoped that Irishmen North and South might manage to adopt a more conciliatory attitude towards each other. Secondly, he felt that something more than mere assurances of the good intentions of Catholics towards Protestants was necessary to reassure Ulster Protestant fears, however imaginary he held those fears to be. In contrast to de Valera he explicitly recognised that the Constitution would have to be revised before, not after, unification. He did not expect unionists to trust in good-will. He told the Oxford Union in 1959:

> We recognise, however, that the fears of Northern Ireland Protestants still exist and that it is unlikely that they could be removed by assurances of good intentions alone, no matter how sincere or how authoritatively expressed. An arrangement which would give them effective power to protect themselves, very especially in regard to educational and religious matters, must clearly be an essential part of any ultimate agreement.

Lemass himself went further. He came to feel that the confessional ethos of the southern Irish state, as enshrined in de Valera's Constitution, should be changed in the interests of genuine republicanism, and not simply as part of a grudging package deal with Ulster Unionists.

Éamon de Valera could not formally meet his Northern Irish counterpart, as it would confer a de facto recognition on the Northern Prime Minister. Sean Lemass had no such problems. The Lemass/O'Neill meeting in 1965. As events turned out it was O'Neill who had more to lose.

He set up an all-party committee on the Constitution, on which he himself served, and which recommended significant revisions in the ethos of the Constitution in 1967. But by that stage Lemass had resigned as Taoiseach. His successor, Jack Lynch, brought a different style of leadership to Irish politics. The recommendations were shelved. Lemass had tried to sow seeds where de Valera would sow none. Only time would tell whether they had fallen on fertile ground and which, if any, would bear ultimate fruit.

Chapter 4

The Price of Independence

That Ireland which we dreamed of would be the home of a people who valued material wealth only as the basis of right living, of a people who were satisfied with frugal comfort and devoted their leisure to the things of the spirit – a land whose countryside would be bright with cosy homesteads, whose fields and villages would be joyous with the sounds of industry, with the romping of sturdy children, the contests of athletic youths and the laughter of comely maidens, whose firesides would be forums for the wisdom of serene old age. It would, in a word, be the home of a people living the life that God desires that man should live.

This most celebrated of all de Valera's evocations of his ideal society, delivered in his St Patrick's Day broadcast of 1943, eloquently conveys his vision of the Ireland of his dreams. It was a far cry from the stark reality. After ten years of de Valera government, 25,000 Irish men and women a year were leaving the country, and more than another 100,000 were swelling the dole queues. The Second World War was aggravating the harsh conditions, but it did not create them. It seemed a long way from that other St Patrick's Day, only ten years before, in the first flush of a famous Fianna Fáil election victory in 1933, when de Valera assured Irish emigrants in London that "We shall not rest until we have lifted the doom of exile which so long has lain upon hundreds of thousands of Irishmen in every generation." Now de Valera was

GOVERNMENT
BY THE RICH
AND
FOR THE RICH

VOTE FOR FIANNA FAIL

shovelling out the Irish as quickly as Britain would take them. They were no longer exiles from malevolent British rule in Ireland, but refugees from a sovereign government. When de Valera looked into his own heart now, the main highway he could see was the road to Dun Laoghaire pier. Why did the reality fall so far short of his ideal?

De Valera came to power in 1932 dedicated to the achievement of the "ultimate aims" of Fianna Fáil contained in the founding Charter of the party in 1926. In the social and economic sphere, the party had three main "ultimate aims". Firstly, "the development of a social system in which, *as far as possible*, equal opportunity will be afforded to every Irish citizen to live a noble and useful Christian life". Secondly, "the distribution of the land of Ireland so as to get the greatest number *possible* of Irish families rooted in the soil of Ireland". Thirdly, "the making of Ireland an economic unit, as self contained and self sufficient *as possible* – with *a proper balance* between agriculture and other *essential* industries" (my emphases).

The general ideology inspiring these aims is clear enough. But the small print must be read too. None of the aims contains an unqualified commitment. They all take refuge in de Valera's favourite escape clause, "as far as possible". "As far as possible" is a very elastic concept. Who decides what is possible? What was "a proper balance" between agriculture and industry and what was an "essential" industry? Who would make these crucial decisions? The "ultimate aims" might pull in votes, but they gave few clues to policy-makers on how to translate the objectives into reality. Nevertheless, de Valera had sufficient faith in these ideals to make a valiant effort to put at least bits of them into practice

1932 election poster. Fianna Fáil were able to capitalise on the unpopularity of umann na nGaedheal's harsh economic policies.

when he came to power in 1932. He seemed particularly solicitous for the small farmer. This contrasted fairly sharply with the approach adopted by the Cumann na nGaedheal government of Mr W. T. Cosgrave since 1922. The agricultural policy of that government was particularly associated with the Minister for Agriculture, Patrick Hogan, an able administrator, a coherent thinker, and an acidulous speaker, who once described his policy as intended to help the fellow who helped himself and to let the other fellow go to the devil. De Valera drew no such distinction between the successful and the unsuccessful, or between the efficient and the inefficient. He subordinated the apparently ruthless economic criterion of Hogan to a broader concept of the social significance of rooting as many families "as possible" on the land. Hogan's policy was based on the assumption that the best market for the Irish farmer was the British market. De Valera preferred to think of Irish agriculture catering primarily for the home market, rather than producing mainly for export. Hogan had no objection to Ireland importing some of her food, if that was cheaper than producing it at home. De Valera detested the thought of Ireland importing most of her wheat requirements, or exporting most of her cattle, simply because that seemed to be the most profitable policy for the farmer in the short term. He subscribed to the ideal of self-sufficiency, and therefore insisted that Ireland should produce her own wheat, even if it was dearer, because this was a more manly thing to do. Irish consumers would admittedly pay more for their bread, but the wheat policy would allegedly employ more agricultural workers. Dearer bread was a small price to pay for this. He therefore launched a tillage campaign under the immediate direction of Jim Ryan, his Minister for Agriculture. The policy tended to assume the character of a vendetta against cattle, based on the conviction that the British market was gone for ever, as de Valera prematurely prophesied in 1933. When de Valera withheld the land annuities, the repayments of the monies which the British government had advanced under the Land Acts of the late nineteenth and early twentieth centuries, to enable tenants to buy out their holdings from the landlords, the British retaliated in 1932 by slapping duties on imports from Ireland. The "economic war" led to a spate of reprisals on both sides, between two bad-tempered governments, both apparently intent on cutting off their noses to spite their faces.

De Valera lost the strictly economic war. Farmers did

Seán Lemass was first elected to Dáil Éireann in a by-election in 1924. His role in the establishment and development of Fianna Fáil was crucial.

not switch from livestock to tillage. Insofar as they switched at all, it was simply from unsubsidised tillage to
subsidised tillage. And tillage in any case no longer
seemed to provide more employment than cattle. The
province that most increased its wheat acreage during
the 1930s, Leinster, also experienced the sharpest drop
in the number of agricultural labourers. Cattle refused
to bow the knee, and accounted for an even higher
proportion of Irish exports in 1939 than in 1932. But de
Valera proved himself adept at plucking political victory
from economic defeat. At home, he succeeded in out-
facing the Blueshirts, who attracted considerable support
from strong farmers who were infuriated by the losses
inflicted, in their view unnecessarily and even wantonly,
by the economic war. Abroad, he skilfully turned the
international political situation to good use and managed
to salvage a diplomatic triumph in his negotiations with
Britain in 1938. In the Anglo-Irish Agreement of that
year, which he had sought in the first instance, he abandoned his vendetta against cattle as British fifth column-
ists, allowing them to be rehabilitated as worthy citizens
of the Irish agricultural world. But he also extracted from
Neville Chamberlain, the British Prime Minister, major
concessions on the land annuities question. The outstanding annuities, to the value of about £100,000,000,
were cancelled in return for a lump-sum payment of only
£10,000,000. By securing the return of the ports from a
Chamberlain harassed by German, Italian and Japanese
threats, and therefore resolved to buy off the Irish problem by concessions, de Valera made it possible for Ireland
to pursue a policy of neutrality in the Second World War.

The 1938 Agreement helped de Valera win the general
election that year, when Fianna Fáil more than recovered

The Irish Free State had terrible housing problems. Fianna Fáil in government
initiated a major housing drive. This helped consolidate urban working class
support.

The housing drive also provided some much needed employment. Building
workers in Cork 1937.

THE ECONOMIC WAR IS ENDED

—

Ireland to Take Over Coast Defence Stations

—

BRITAIN TO GET £10,000,000 IN FINAL SETTLEMENT

—

Special Duties and Customs Emergency Duties to be Abolished

The Dominion
Malcolm Macd
Downing st

FROM "

(BY SPECIAL

THE AG

—

The end of the Economic War in 1938 threatened the virtual monopoly enjoyed by many Irish manufacturers protected from competition by high tariffs. However, the war soon came and new and more pressing problems arose.

the losses it had sustained in the 1937 Election, and returned to power with an overall majority once more. It is hard to assess what impact the Agreement might have had on the economic situation. The Second World War intervened so soon that it is difficult to discern what trends might have developed in normal circumstances. The Agreement was intended to mark the end of a particular phase in agricultural policy. On the face of it, it seemed to promise some gains for livestock producers, who stood to regain more favourable access to the British market. But that improvement in their prospects was achieved only by the quid pro quo of opening the possibility of better access for British industrial products to the Irish market. To that extent, it seemed to some

136

observers to have jeopardised the industrial progress of the previous six years.

That progress was largely the result of the industrialisation drive launched by Seán Lemass, de Valera's chief lieutenant in industrial affairs. Lemass faced a daunting challenge when he became Minister for Industry and Commerce in 1932. The economy was already plunged into slump as a result of the great international depression that had begun in 1929. Neither management nor workers were geared up for the challenge of an industrialisation policy. There was a desperate dearth of private enterprise in the classic sense. Many civil servants, and particularly the Department of Finance under its formidable secretary, J. J. McElligott, were highly sceptical of the industrialisation drive. They were particularly suspicious of, and indeed hostile to, the policy of protection long advocated by Fianna Fáil and quickly implemented by Lemass. The Cumann na nGaedheal government had adopted some protectionist measures, but only on a trial and error basis. It was singularly devoid of any ideological commitment to protection, on either economic or social grounds. Cumann na nGaedheal did adopt an increasing number of protectionist measures in late 1931 in the face of the international slump, as dumping increased. But it did so reluctantly, almost as a sinner against the light, not as a giant leap forward on the path to economic redemption.

Pursuing an industrialisation policy at a time of buoyant international markets might have seemed to have held out some prospects of success. Launching an industrialisation drive in a period of intense depression seemed to many a hopeless, even a suicidal, prospect.

The economic war that immediately broke out over the annuities issue reduced yet further the size of the home market by depressing farmers' incomes even below the level imposed by falling prices on the British market. The economic war therefore exacerbated the problems confronting Lemass, but it did not create them. These problems seemed insurmountable to faint hearts even before the economic war. But the Department of Industry and Commerce was no place for faint hearts in the 1930s. Many risks had to be taken, and many mistakes were inevitably made while Lemass and the outstanding new Secretary of his Department, John Leydon, learned their trade. In the difficult circumstances, however, they achieved remarkable success. There were only 110,000 workers in industrial employment in 1932, but by 1938 there were 166,000. The number of industrial jobs expanded by 50 per cent in six years, a quite unprecedented achievement, even making all due allowance for the low level from which the rise began. Where private enterprise could not cope with the challenge, Lemass either established or expanded the "semi-state" sector to grasp latent opportunities. The best-known examples include the Irish Sugar Company, in 1933, the Turf Development Board (which later became Bórd na Móna) in 1934, and Aer Lingus in 1936.

Despite all the doubts, difficulties, and mistakes, much was achieved in those hectic early years of the Fianna Fáil administration. But Lemass had to run hard in order to stand still. Unemployment would have been significantly worse but for his policy. Nevertheless, it remained stubbornly high, and emigration rates in the later 1930s showed little improvement over those of the mid-1920s. The housing drive resulted in the construction or renovation of 132,000 houses between 1932 and 1942, the highest level in many decades. The social problems of the giant new complexes rising up around

Dublin lay happily hidden in the future, and the new housing drive, which began at long last to clear the foul slums which had scarred the face of urban Ireland, must count as the most impressive of all the social achievements of the decade. In addition, de Valera brought a genuine compassion, however much it may have been reinforced by electoral considerations, to the plight of the poorest and most defenceless sections of the community. Not only did his administration extend and increase unemployment benefit, but it also increased Old Age Pensions, and introduced Widows' and Orphans' Pensions from 1934. However meagre the rates paid seem from a retrospective viewpoint, they brought some relief to those most in need of it.

The first flush of success had begun to fade by 1937. There simply wasn't the money to finance the social and economic policy any longer. De Valera himself conceded privately that he was at his wits' end in economic and social matters, and didn't know where to turn next. The housing drive began to slow down. The protectionist policy could already be seen to be storing up problems in the present, not to mention the future. Many of the new firms were guaranteed virtual monopoly positions behind high tariff barriers, or through severe quota restrictions on imports. They felt they didn't have to bother greatly about efficiency. They looked forward to permanent protection at the expense not only of the foreign producer, but of the domestic tax-payer and the consumer, who had to pay higher prices for poor quality goods to keep these firms in existence. Profiteering became so blatant that Lemass had to establish the Prices Commission in 1938 to try to provide some sort of control over manufacturers anxious to exploit the defenceless consumer.

The Prices Commission faced all the familiar problems confronted by government agencies when trying to influence prices in the private sphere. Its creation acknowledged the problem, but hardly solved it. Lemass therefore inevitably began to think of ways of reducing protection, of retreating from the full protectionist programme, in order to spur employers towards a search for greater efficiency by exposing them to the threat of competition from imports. The problem, of course, was that jobs would be lost if Irish employers failed to respond to the challenge. Manufacturers knew that the government could hardly dare to abandon the protectionist policy to which it was so ideologically committed and which still appeared to be the only hope of creating employment. But Lemass was determined to do something. The Anglo-Irish Trade Agreement in 1938 equipped him with one possible weapon, by making provision for the reconsideration of tariff and quota levels with respect to British industrial products.

Lemass would have been sorely tempted to use his powers to threaten recalcitrant Irish manufacturers with the consequences. It would have been most interesting to have seen what would have happened had the war not broken out in 1939. Irish manufacturers were well aware of the dangers to themselves. They protested bitterly at the government's failure to consult them on the terms of the Agreement. And in the short space between the Agreement and the outbreak of the war, Lemass began to speak a new language, which sent a thrill of fear through many of the employers and workers in the firms he had called into being. This was the strange, alien, heretical language of efficiency. Protection, he now chose to stress, was not an end in itself. It was merely a means towards the end of creating an efficient industrial base.

If Irish industry were to expand further, it must export. It could only export if it were efficient. It could not therefore be protected or pampered for much longer. "It was never conceived as possible", he told unsympathetic businessmen,

> That the state could be made completely independent of foreign trade or locked in a watertight compartment cut off from the current of international life .... Now their industries had passed beyond the infancy stage and were capable of facing comparison with industries in other countries, and they would have to be prepared to face that comparison.

Lemass in 1939 frequently sounded like the Lemass of 1959. More unlikely apostles of the strange new doctrine of efficiency also surfaced, however fleetingly. The *Irish Press* warned businessmen in 1939 that Irish industry should now "be reasonably expected to stand on its own feet .... The era of spoon feeding is over."

Lemass was determined to try to make Irish industry competitive. There was in him a certain streak of the puritan ethic contempt for the sloucher and the second-rater. De Valera took a different, and perhaps a broader view, of human nature. His ideal was one of "balance", both within economic affairs, and between economic and other aspects of human activity. The idea of an integrated personality, both individual personality and collective national personality, took precedence over economic efficiency. The "ultimate aims" of Fianna Fáil spoke of "a proper *balance* [my emphasis] between agriculture and the other essential industries". In 1939 de Valera told the Dáil that "no policy is going to give perfection: there is going to be a certain amount of evil attached to every policy, and it is a question of the balance of advantages and evils and the taking of the best from the national point of view." This was itself a concession to critics of protectionist ideology. He was, by implication at least, conceding that even protectionism had "a certain amount of evil" attached to it. Balance is a word that recurs regularly in his rhetoric. But he didn't seem to have any very clear idea of how balance was to be achieved. The problem with his "balance" was that it seemed to be resulting in unbalance, or imbalance, by 1938-39, as the emigrants continued to flock out, singularly unimpressed with the "balance" achieved. De Valera was also a great believer in taking the long-term view. "Ultimately" was as favourite a word of his as was balance. Lemass, responsible for solving short-term problems, was unable to afford the luxury of thinking in terms of "ultimate" solutions. "Ultimate" success would not put meals on the table, or build houses, or find jobs for the unemployed.

Fairly sharp differences of emphasis can therefore be detected between the approaches of de Valera and Lemass on the eve of the Second World War. Even de Valera, however, did begin to mouth the new term, efficiency, from time to time. He did, nevertheless, concede a certain conflict between the ideals of efficiency and self-sufficiency. He conceded to the Dáil in 1939:

> I am admitting that we cannot have it both ways; if we go in for efficient production, the principle drawback is that we have not as big a market as people in other countries and therefore we cannot produce per unit as efficiently as they can. However, we have the brains and the skill to produce for ourselves.

This was of course to obscure the issue. Several "people in other countries" had very small domestic markets.

Seán Lemass electioneering in 1948. After the war Lemass realised that there could be no going back to the policies of the 1930s. The electorate felt that too and put Fianna Fáil out of office.

Women in Connemara in 1947. Many Irish women chose an alternative to Éamon de Valera's view of their role. They emigrated.

The Scandinavian countries and Switzerland come immediately to mind. Many small continental countries envied Ireland its potentially free access to "as big a market" as Britain. By confining his implied comparison to big countries, de Valera evaded the main criticisms of his "self-sufficiency" policy. The problem with "self-sufficiency" was that many of the selfs were not satisfied with the sufficiency. De Valera once said that when the serf came out of the castle he had to be satisfied with cottage fare. Many of the mere Irish were not prepared to accept the cottage standards de Valera considered good enough for them. For better or for worse, wisely or foolishly, they insisted on flying from the cottage back in the direction of the castle. De Valera's relaxed attitude towards efficiency could be detected in the Constitution of 1937, where he included a clause to the effect that

> the state shall endeavour to secure that private enterprise shall be so conducted as to ensure reasonable efficiency in the production and distribution of goods and has to protect the public against unjust exploitation.

What was "reasonable" efficiency? Who defined it? And who defined "unjust" exploitation as distinct from "just" exploitation? This clause was hardly a clarion call to competitive efficiency. It spread a capacious constitutional cloak over the laggards in the race, so long as their bungling did not become too blatant.

Lemass had little time for philosophising on the concept of "reasonable" efficiency. He wanted quick results. But he failed to find a solution that would combine efficiency with expanding employment. Competitive efficiency on international markets was not a priority during the Second World War, when the problem was much more how to import than how to export. After the war Lemass proposed a drastic scheme to improve industrial efficiency, as he found himself plagued by the same problems that preoccupied him in 1939. He opted for a sweepingly interventionist solution. He proposed that, in the last resort, the Department of Industry and Commerce should have the authority to nationalise, at least *de facto*, any firm in the country that failed to meet standards of efficiency prescribed by his own inspectors. It was certainly one of the most radical, and many critics considered it one of the most reckless, schemes ever suggested by a senior minister. Lemass did claim that in practice it would not be necessary to implement the threat. The very fear of a take-over would, he held, spur recalcitrant businessmen to greater effort. Nevertheless, his Cabinet colleagues understandably took fright at this ambitious proposal. They watered it down, and a very modified version went before the Dáil as the Industrial Prices and Efficiency Bill in 1947. The whole project lapsed when Fianna Fáil lost office after the general election of 1948.

It was his wartime experience, when he served as both Minister for Supplies and Minister for Industry and Commerce, and had at his disposal a fleet of inspectors trying to ensure public conformity to wartime regulations, that suggested to Lemass the possibility of an inspectorate for imposing efficiency in the post-war period. The energy and ingenuity of Lemass as Minister for Supplies, again ably backed by John Leydon, and by a cadre of bright young civil servants, consolidated his reputation as the ablest member of the Cabinet. But he faced a daunting situation. The war taught the prophets of self-sufficiency a painful lesson in elementary economics. Back in 1928 de Valera lamented that "we will, unfortunately, not be able to cut ourselves completely

off" from the world economy. He would have liked to have seen the country "surrounded by a wall" and prophesied that "if by any chance we were cut off .... I am satisfied that we could here, now, in this country, maintain a population two or three times the size of our present population." Lemass, too, had once appeared to subscribe to the doctrine of self-sufficiency. As we have seen, he was already busy on a new script before 1939. But he had little time to learn the lines, before de Valera's dream of a dozen years before came true in 1940. Ireland was cut off. De Valera's dream became a nightmare for Lemass. Where Lemass had spent the previous seven years desperately trying to stop imports, he spent the war years desperately trying to increase them. Industrialisation had reduced rather than increased self-sufficiency. It made imported raw materials more important than ever. As those raw materials were cut off during the war, production at home inevitably suffered. Industrial output fell 25 per cent. Only large-scale emigration kept unemployment in check. The government actually suspended tariffs in 1942 when Ireland became a virtually full free-trading economy once more. Unfortunately, there were precious few goods to trade freely in. War gave de Valera a good deal more self-sufficiency than he bargained for. The saga of Irish Shipping Ltd, set up in 1941 to loosen to some extent Ireland's total dependence on British shipping, cannot disguise the fact that supplies to Ireland remained almost wholly dependent on British goodwill throughout the war. "Sovereignty" proved an elusive objective in economic matters. The rhetoric was much more consoling than the reality.

The early 1950s were a period of massive emigration, high unemployment and no economic growth. It was time to puncture the balloon of inherited illusions.

By the late 1950s it was accepted that the Irish market was too small to support full employment. If jobs were to be found for the unemployed then it was necessary to produce for export. That meant being competitive.

If the war posed a new set of economic headaches for the government, and particularly for Lemass, it came as a Godsend to the businessmen who felt threatened by the chilling doctrine of efficiency in 1939. Businessmen were now automatically protected from the threat of foreign competition. If production fell because of the lack of raw materials and the contraction in the size of the home market, wartime profiteering offered some compensation. A lively black market flourished, with varying degrees of official connivance, and despite the plethora of inspectors mobilised by Lemass.

The black market made modest fortunes for those with an eye to the main chance. But it scarcely prepared the economy, limping its way through the war, for adjustment to post-war circumstances. In comparison with the public expectations, the economy recovered only haltingly between 1945 and 1948, when it still proved unable to offer an acceptable standard of living to many of its people. Neither Fianna Fáil nor the inter-party governments under John A. Costello, which held office between 1948 and 1951, and again between 1954 and 1957, managed to solve the traditional economic problems of the period. The Minister for Finance in the first inter-party government, Patrick McGilligan, took some enterprising initiatives, but they failed to come to fruition at the time. Daniel Morrissey, the inter-party Minister for Industry and Commerce, launched the Industrial Development Authority, which would in later years come to play a major role in stimulating economic growth. But that still lay long in the future in 1949. Seán MacBride, Minister for External Affairs and leader of Clann na Poblachta, sponsored a number of radical thrusts, but failed to carry most of them through. Lemass in his turn fought to persuade Fianna Fáil to adopt more expansionist policies when the party returned to power between 1951 and 1954. But he found himself frustrated by the growing conservatism of de Valera, and by the dogged resistance from an ageing Cabinet, especially the doughty Seán MacEntee, whom de Valera had reappointed as Minister for Finance between 1951 and 1954. The redoubtable J. J. McElligott remained Secretary of Finance until 1953, and continued to resist the Lemass heresies with all the devotion of a high priest of orthodoxy. It wasn't until Fianna Fáil returned to office in 1957 that Lemass finally broke free from the bonds that had pinned him down during the previous decade. Now, circumstances were at last propitious for the acceptance of his brand of leadership.

Lemass was fortunate in several respects in the timing of his succession to de Valera. The inter-party government between 1954 and 1957 began to reduce the role allocated to protection in the economy by introducing a variety of tax incentives for industry which Lemass would adopt and expand. In his groping for an alternative to protection to foster efficiency, he now grasped the potential of this new approach. In addition, the depth of the economic crisis of the mid-1950s convinced even the Department of Finance, especially its ablest member, the young T. K. Whitaker, that desperate remedies were called for, at least by Irish standards. Emigration had now reached 50,000 a year. The phrase "the vanishing Irish" became fashionable. If this was to be the verdict on nearly forty years of self-government, it would be a bleak commentary indeed on the capacity of the Irish to manage their own affairs. It had been the custom to argue, in the Civil Service, that the flood of emigration after the Second World War had little objective economic cause. Conservative commentators preferred to attribute this outflow to some peculiar psychic quirk in the Irish, and particularly in Irish women, who were now flocking out in ever-growing numbers, allegedly turning their backs on good prospects in Ireland.

De Valera had a very clear role in mind for the girls in his ideal Ireland. They had value only as mothers. They had none as individuals. In his Constitution of 1937 they were firmly kept in their place in the kitchen and the breeding room. The much-quoted clauses of Article 41 defined woman's role quite clearly.

Article 41, 2.1: In particular, the state recognises that by her life within the home, woman gives to the state a support without which the common good cannot be achieved.

2.2: The state shall, therefore, endeavour to ensure that mothers shall not be obliged by economic necessity to engage in labour to the neglect of their duties in the home.

The message was clear. Once woman (or was it mother? – the two seem to be used interchangeably) ventured outside the door, she ceased to fulfil her duty.

In practice, the girls increasingly turned their backs on de Valera's dream Ireland. In 1926 the last census before de Valera came to power showed that there was a big surplus of girls in rural areas compared with the number of young farmers. By the time de Valera finally resigned in 1959, the census was already recording a severe shortage of girls compared with the number of young farmers. The "comely maidens" whom de Valera rapturously invoked in his 1943 Patrick's Day address sabotaged his Mass and may pole, or buttermilk and bog hole, image of an ideal Ireland. They were not amused by the vision of

When Éamon de Valera became President in 1959 Seán Lemass became Taoiseach. In 1961 Lemass fought and won a general election as Taoiseach.

the "serene old age" they might spend as "forums of wisdom" by the fireside of his imagination.

The irony was that it was not because they rejected de Valera's ideal, but because they embraced it, that the girls emigrated. No society in Europe so exalted the ideal of the family in its official rhetoric. None in practice deprived so many young people of the right to marry by the simple but effective device of denying them an inheritance. The small farmer, de Valera's ideal Irishman, reared his daughters for export. The Irish girls who flocked out after 1945 did not emigrate with the "ultimate aim" of becoming career women. They emigrated rather to enjoy the right their own society denied them, the right to a family. They accepted, by and large, that their place was in the kitchen and in the bedroom. But there were not enough kitchens or bedrooms for them. They would have stayed at home if de Valera could have delivered the goods. He couldn't.

De Valera had gone to considerable lengths to incorporate in the Constitution his general ideas concerning the nature of a just society in Ireland. He could not, of course, enshrine the "ultimate aims" of Fianna Fáil, as enunciated in 1926, in the Constitution and make them legally binding, subject only to the interpretation of the courts. That would have exposed him to the vulgar charge of party politics. He struck on an astute alternative. He chose to include "Directive Principles of Social Policy" as Article 45. That article contained impeccable sentiments.

> The principles of social policy set forth in this Article are intended for the general guidance of the Oireáchtas. The application of those principles in the making of laws shall be the care of the Oireachtas exclusively, and shall not be cognizable by any Court under any of the provisions of this Constitution.
>
> 1: The State shall strive to promote the welfare of the whole people by securing and protecting as effectively as it may a social order in which justice and charity shall inform all the institutions of the national life.
>
> 2: The State shall, in particular, direct its policy towards securing
>
> i. That the citizens (all of whom, men and women equally, have the right to an adequate means of livelihood) may through their occupations find the means of making reasonable provisions for their domestic needs.

ii. That the ownership and control of the material resources of the community may be so distributed amongst private individuals and the various classes as best to subserve the common good.

iii. That, especially, the operation of free competition shall not be allowed so to develop as to result in the concentration of the ownership or control of essential commodities in a few individuals to the common detriment.

iv. That in what pertains to the control of credit the constant and predominant aim shall be the welfare of the people as a whole.

v. That there may be established on the land in economic security as many families as in the circumstances shall be practicable.

3, 1: The State shall favour and, where necessary, supplement private initiative in industry and commerce.

3, 2: The State shall endeavour to secure that private enterprise shall be so conducted as to ensure reasonable efficiency in the production and distribution of goods and as to protect the public against unjust exploitation.

4, 1: The State pledges itself to safeguard with especial care the economic interests of the weaker sections of the community and, where necessary, to contribute to the support of the infirm, the widow, the orphan, and the aged.

4, 2: The State shall endeavour to ensure that the strength and health of workers, men and women, and the tender age of children shall not be abused and that citizens shall not be forced by economic necessity to enter avocations unsuited to their sex, age or strength.

Only a boor would really be so churlish as to oppose such admirable sentiments. But how could they be implemented? Who was to interpret the degree of "justice and charity" in "all the institutions of the national life" (and what were they?); who defined "reasonable provision for their domestic needs", or "the common good", or "essential commodities", or "where necessary"? Who were "the weaker sections of the community"? Would they include, for instance, "the infirm, the widow, the orphan, and the aged" at the mercy of wildcat strikers?

The escape clause came in the introduction to Article 45. The article bound absolutely nobody. It was not part of the Constitution in any legal sense. It was merely "intended for the general guidance of the Oireachtas", and "the application of those principles in the making of laws shall be the care of the Oireachtas exclusively, and shall not be cognisable by any court under any of the provisions of this Constitution". De Valera was himself perfectly sincere about the general thrust of these "Directive Principles". Readers must decide for themselves how seriously they have been taken by the Oireachtas, or how far they represent the codification of collective national hypocrisy.

The Directive Principles were contemptuously ignored by the senior Civil Service, particularly by the Department of Finance, when they happened to clash with real life. In 1946 J. J. McElligott would point out frostily to the then Minister for Finance, Frank Aiken, who was so careless as to quote Article 45.2.iv to the effect "that in what pertains to the control of credit the constant and predominant aim shall be the welfare of the people as a whole", that those lofty sentiments meant precisely nothing. All that mattered were the directions contained

in the Central Bank Act of 1942, against which the
sentiments of the Directive Principles were powerless
and indeed meaningless. For who was to define "the
welfare of the people as a whole" in this context?

By 1957 it was clear to anyone who wished to see that
the Directive Principles directed nothing, and that de
Valera's dream of 1943, if taken seriously, was a prescrip-
tion for disaster. The "contests of athletic youths" were
indeed taking place – on the building sites of London
and Birmingham. "The laughter of comely maidens"
was heard now in the nurses' homes or the typing pools
of England. Whitaker, the new Secretary of the Department of Finance, and Lemass, who at last dominated
economic policy virtually unimpeded on his return to
office in 1957, even before he became Taoiseach in 1959,
decided to puncture the balloon of inherited illusions.
Whitaker's famous report, *Economic Development*, published in November 1958, enjoyed so historic an impact
partly at least because it recognised reality. Whitaker
did not waste words berating the natives for daring to
emigrate from God's own country. He acknowledged
the Irish were emigrating because there was nothing
satisfactory for them at home, not because of some innate
perversity. Lemass too believed that desperate situations
called for desperate remedies. Indeed, his critics would
say that he believed that ordinary situations called for
desperate remedies. Whitaker and Lemass found more
receptivity to the new approach than might have been
the case even a few years before because it was now
difficult for even the most complacent to deny that the
country faced a potentially catastrophic economic crisis.
For at least a brief spell, "necessity" permitted an
approach that might have roused fierce resistance in less
critical circumstances. Lemass jettisoned not only many

of the specific policies with which he himself was earlier associated, but more importantly the whole mentality intimately associated with the age of de Valera.

Lemass himself had never shared de Valera's dream of a small farmers' Utopia. De Valera was reared in an agricultural labourer's cottage. To him, the security of the small farm represented the grasping ambition of his ancestral class. Lemass, Dublin born and bred, had no feeling of romantic nostalgia for small-farm Ireland. The only surplus he saw coming off small farms was children. Small farmers could not produce, in his view, the surpluses necessary to build up a thriving economy. The whole thrust of his policy after 1932 suggests that he shared the ideal vigorously expressed by Professor John Busteed of University College, Cork, one of the few economists to detect some merit in Fianna Fáil policy in the 1930s:

> A nation condemned to peasant specialisation in farming is doomed to be a nation of hewers of wood and drawers of water, no matter what improvement may be effected in production and marketing efficiency by the farmers. Ireland's hope then rests in making the greatest possible effort and in carrying the heaviest possible burden to promote industrialisation.

Lemass considered industrialisation to be the only hope of keeping the Irish at home. It was the only way jobs could be provided. His industrialisation policy after 1932 was inevitably subversive of de Valera's arcadian ideal. How then did two such different personalities, with such conflicting visions, ever come to work in harness? One answer may be that de Valera ultimately sacrificed his concept of an ideal Irish society to the overriding concept of economic sovereignty. Lemass persuaded de Valera that only through industrialisation

'hree successive Fianna Fáil holders of the office of Taoiseach, Seán Lemass, ack Lynch and Charles Haughey. On this occasion in 1965 they were going to ondon for trade talks.

could Ireland become "self-sufficient and self-contained as an economic unit", an embalmed "ultimate aim" of Fianna Fáil. This principle inevitably conflicted with another "ultimate aim", "the distribution of the land of Ireland so as to get the greatest number possible of Irish families rooted in the soil of Ireland". "The greatest number possible" became a very shrinking figure as industrialisation proceeded. If industrialisation succeeded it would not, ultimately, create a balance with rural Ireland. It would destroy rural Ireland. Lemass would have replied that rural Ireland, like comparable rural societies everywhere, was doomed anyway. The only question was whether a post-rural Ireland would succeed it, or whether the decay of rural Ireland would drag Ireland into the mire with it. What de Valera privately felt as his early hopes failed to materialise remains speculative. But it may be noted that the Land Commission, which was charged with redistributing land so as to root as many families as possible in the soil, slowed down its operations significantly after the mid-thirties.

Lemass was as committed to self-sufficiency as de Valera. But he developed a radically different concept of self-sufficiency. For de Valera, self-sufficiency meant that Ireland should be protected from competition, that it should ideally have a wall around it. Lemass felt, or quickly came to feel, that that was impossible. Self-sufficiency could only come, ultimately, from efficiency – from the ability to take on all comers in open competition. Self-sufficiency meant self reliance, not protection. For de Valera, protection was almost an end in itself: for Lemass it was merely a means to an end. Now, by 1957, that means was patently failing to deliver the end. He calculated that Ireland needed at least 15,000 new jobs a year to absorb the emigrants. A maximum of 2,000 a year was being created behind the protectionist barriers. What was the solution?

Once before Lemass had made a supreme effort to persuade de Valera that Fianna Fáil should embark on a programme of ambitious economic planning. He pointed out in 1942, perhaps inspired by the warnings of F. H. Boland, that Ireland might face at the end of the war the challenge of 400,000 returned emigrants and discharged soldiers. Only a monumental effort at job creation could avoid chaos and even social disintegration. Lemass wanted a Ministry of Labour to be established with draconian powers for the direction of labour in Irish society. He also demanded a plan to co-ordinate every aspect of economic activity in the country. De Valera responded by going so far as to set up a Cabinet Committee on Economic Planning in 1942. It met nearly sixty times over the next two years. But de Valera did not share his Minister's sense of urgency. He soon began to use the committee to suffocate Lemass, to prevent measures as drastic as those Lemass was demanding. As it became clear in 1943 and 1944 that Britain herself intended embarking on major reconstruction programmes after the war and that Irish labour was unlikely to come flocking back, all sense of urgency disappeared. The Committee on Economic Planning, which Lemass had hoped would guide the economy on a new path in the post-war years, actually ceased to meet at the end of the war. It wasn't until the crisis of 1956-7 that a similar spirit of urgency could be rekindled and Lemass finally got his chance.

In 1957 Lemass was older and wiser than fifteen years before. Nevertheless, he still had a penchant for the big throw. In contrast to the normally cautious and conserv-

Prosperity came to Ireland in the 1960s. For some the move was but a few steps. It still left Ireland way behind European levels of achievement.

ative de Valera, Lemass had an impetuous streak in him, which tended instinctively to opt for extreme solutions to problems. Part of Whitaker's design may have been to channel the potentially reckless energy of Lemass into what he considered to be coherent channels.

Lemass faced a tricky political problem in finding an alternative to protection. Efficiency was all very well, just as well as it had been in 1939, until it hurt Fianna Fáil's friends. Many of the businessmen who flourished behind the protectionist wall of the 1930s had become devout supporters of the party. How could Lemass now pull the rug from under their feet? He would face bitter internal political battles if he seemed to be reneging on loyal supporters of the party. The shift from protection

160

to free trade is always a politically delicate one, given the range of vested interests involved. It was probably very much in Lemass's interest that he was able to take his initiatives under the protective umbrella of de Valera, still hovering overhead as party leader until 1959. Lemass struck on an astute political compromise, building partly on the initiatives of the preceding inter-party government which he now moulded in his own image.

The Lemass compromise was to import efficiency through offering incentives to foreign firms to bring their managerial talent, their know-how and their marketing connections to Ireland. They would, he hoped, manufacture the exports that Ireland so desperately needed. But they would not pose an immediate threat to the protected sector. Their incentives would be for export only, not for production for the home market. The protected sector would therefore gain a breathing space to try to put its house in order. Lemass established Committees of Industrial Organisation in 1961 and 1962 to examine the efficiency of the protected sectors. These came close to what he had in mind fifteen years before with his Industrial Efficiency proposals, but now he relied much more on the carrot of incentives, grants, etc. and not at all on the stick of threatened nationalisation, to persuade reluctant employers to improve efficiency. It wasn't until the Anglo-Irish Trade Agreement of 1965 that free trade was to become a reality, and then not fully for ten years. Lemass reckoned that by then the protected sector would have had nearly twenty years' warning of the necessity to become competitive. It seems doubtful if he felt disposed to shed many tears over the laggards, whom he may even have come to regard as permanent spongers on the working elements in Irish society.

It was in much the same spirit that Lemass decided

that Ireland must try to become a member of the new European Economic Community in 1961. The Irish application lapsed when Charles de Gaulle vetoed the British application in 1963. But Lemass made it clear that Ireland would continue pressing for entry as soon as opportunity offered. De Valera was much more hesitant about "Europe". Lemass, with his conquistador temperament, tended to relish the excitement of a new challenge, even of an apparently daunting one. De Valera, perhaps more worldly wise, and perhaps too with less confidence in the capacity of the Irish to rise to such challenges, was much more cautious. De Valera tended to see dangers where Lemass sensed opportunities. Who was to say which was the wiser? It might be that the Lemass vision could flourish only if the majority of Irishmen were Lemasses. Sceptics would wonder about that. Was the sponger mentality so deeply ingrained in the Irish psyche that Brussels would be seen simply as a new source of handouts? Had the state-sponsored bodies, many of which Lemass had founded, become such labour monopolists that they had threatened to grow into Frankensteins, devouring the sustenance of the mother that gave them suck? Would trade unions, once cast as defenders of the exploited against exploiters, themselves adopt an exploiting role as soon as opportunity offered? De Valera put little faith in human nature, even Irish nature! Lemass tended to be an incorrigible optimist.

A further irony remained. De Valera's dream of his ideal Ireland had few attractions for Lemass. He may even have despised it. He said little about the sanctity of the family, or about the life God meant that men should live. It is indeed remarkable, given the rhetoric of his generation, that he so rarely summoned God to bear witness to his views. Above all, he did not feel what was good for small farmers was good for Ireland. The number of farm families continued to decline in his Ireland, as it had declined in de Valera's. Yet for the first time in a century, the total number of families in Ireland increased during the 1960s. Lemass spoke little about motherhood, an obsession with de Valera that may admittedly have been partly psychological because he lost his own mother so early. Yet the number of mothers in Ireland in the 1960s increased for the first time since the Famine, thanks to the greater opportunities for founding a family created by the success of the new Lemass policy. De Valera's rhetoric did not stop emigration. Lemass's actions did.

In a sense, of course, prosperity came to the Ireland of the sixties without any adequate prior preparation. An ethically shallow society found itself frequently unable to cope in a mature manner with its new-found relative affluence, however far it continued to lag behind the European achievement of the time. The ethics of the gossip-columnist, drooling over the tawdry mediocrity of a socialite Ireland apeing its image of the jet set, enjoyed free rein. But this was not an inevitable response. The economic achievement of the sixties permitted a range of alternative societies to be built on it. Lemass himself resigned in 1966. It would be for the next generation to decide what type of society it wanted. The economic achievement at least ensured that a society could exist. If Lemass were reproached with burying the Ireland of de Valera's dream forever, he might have replied, and with some truth, that de Valera's Ireland was already dead, and that none other than the Chief himself had presided over the obsequies. And that it was only by burying the rotting carcass that a new Ireland could be given hope of life.

Chapter 5

De Valera and the Irish People

The main features of de Valera's idealised Ireland – as adumbrated by him at regular intervals throughout his life, most notably in the celebrated bucolic *aisling* of 1943 – are easily listed. He longed for a sovereign Irish republic, Irish-speaking, based on rural small-holders, self-sufficient in food, with a highly decentralised manufacturing sector providing most of the country's needs in industrial and manufactured goods; a society providing work for its people at home, drawing largely on its own resources (material and spiritual); a society living in frugal comfort and imbued with sound Christian principles. It would not be a land flowing with milk and honey (the ascetic and penitential in Dev would recoil at such dangerous language), but it would feed its own people and furnish them with a vision of social endeavour aimed at achieving contentment in this life and salvation in the next.

The question to be asked at once is, how did Irish society – the actual living community – approximate or compare to this ideal in the five decades after 1922? Or, more specifically, what steps were taken during the de Valera years to realise these ideals? Certainly, looking back from the vantage point of the late fifties, it would be hard to have patience with, let alone belief in, the tableau of Christian contentment outlined by de Valera to an introverted, neutral Ireland in 1943. By the late fifties the very viability of a sovereign Irish state was being widely questioned. Emigration figures were higher than at any time since the 1880s, and this was merely the crisis point of a story of almost continuous population decline since the foundation of the Free State.

Population of 26 Counties

		(in thousands)
1911	—	3,140
1926	—	2,972
1936	—	2,968
1946	—	2,955
1951	—	2,961
1956	—	2,898
1961	—	2,818

Net Emigration from 26 Counties

1926-36	—	166,751
1936-46	—	187,111
1946-51	—	119,568
1956-61	—	212,003

The Irish economy, far from being overwhelmingly self-sufficient, was more fully integrated than ever into the British economy. By 1952, for example, the United Kingdom accounted for almost 90 percent of the value of Irish exports, and for over 50 percent of the value of imports. The country was not Irish-speaking. In fact the Gaeltacht continued to contract in size and numbers, as it had done uninterruptedly since the establishment of an Irish state. And while there were some signs that

It is hard for Irish people today to realise just how great was the economic poverty of the newly independent Irish Free State. A cottage in Donegal.

The only hope of employment for many Irish people lay in emigration. As often with emigration, loneliness and exploitation were to be expected. Charitable agencies did their best but the numbers leaving Ireland were very large.

other aspects of the language revival policy had made progress, it was becoming increasingly clear that doubts were spreading not only about the appropriateness of some of the instruments of the language policy but also about the very definition of the policy itself. In short, the final years of de Valera's active participation in political life were in many respects the most distressful years Irish society had experienced since the 1880s, if not indeed since the great famine.

What went wrong? What happened to the "dream"? Was there ever any real chance that it would become anything more than a dream? Was it, in fact, a dangerous mirage, dooming those beguiled by it to inevitable disappointment and disillusion? Any serious address to these questions must begin with an assessment of what was actually attempted.

The revival of the Irish language as the vernacular of the mass of the people was one of the cardinal objectives of social policy in Ireland in the decades after the establishment of the Free State. Indeed, it was probably the most radical proposal for social reconstruction – the most revolutionary objective in state-building – undertaken by the new state in 1922. De Valera's lifelong devotion to the Irish language and his public evangelism on its behalf has tended to leave many with the impression that most of the major features of the language revival policy were the creation of de Valera and Fianna Fáil. This, however, is simply not the case. A majority of the Sinn Féin élite of 1919-21 shared a strong conviction of the necessity for the revival of Irish. And even after the Treaty split, the

The corner-stone of the language revival policy was the Gaelicisation of the educational system. Children in Donegal.

Despite the goodwill of successive governments the Gaeltacht areas contracted as emigration, social dislocation and the relentless penetration of English made the surviving enclaves more and more vulnerable.

Cumann na nGaedheal government of the twenties contained more than its share of those who had "been to school at the Gaelic League" in the early years of the century. Indeed, it is possible that, precisely because their credentials as nationalists were being disputed, the Cumann na nGaedheal ministers (including such ardent revivalists as Blythe, Mulcahy and Eoin MacNeill) were especially anxious to have a "forward" policy on the language revival. Nor was it merely a matter of shared objectives. The basic strategy for the revival, and the instruments which the government deemed appropriate for its implementation – all of these were laid down in the 1920s. The cornerstone of the strategy was the Gaelicisation of the educational system. In the primary sector, where the government had effective control, measures were introduced to focus the curriculum on the teaching of Irish and on its use as the medium of instruction in the primary schools. The policy was advanced in the secondary sector through exhortation and special incentives, and, above all, by decreeing that Irish be an essential element in state examinations for the Intermediate and Leaving certificates. The training (and retraining) of teachers, the establishment of special preparatory colleges to provide secondary education through Irish for Irish-speaking pupils and to ensure the recruitment of fluent Irish speakers for the teaching profession, and the initiation of a policy to provide for university education through Irish in Galway (in 1929) – these were the main elements of the strategy to Gaelicise the education system. If to these we add the gradual (in some cases very gradual) introduction of Irish into the state bureaucracy, the establishment of a government publication agency (An Gúm) to spearhead the publication of reading material in Irish, the state subvention of an

Irish-speaking theatre, and the general acceptance of the argument (contained in the Report of a special commission in 1925/6) that massive social reconstruction, economic development and sensitive socio-linguistic planning were needed to arrest and reverse the decline of the Gaeltacht, we have before us the main strategy for the language revival pursued by the state for over forty years after 1922. By 1932 this policy was well advanced.

The advent of de Valera and of Fianna Fáil to power in 1932 saw an intensification of this effort in language revival, an increase in the frequency and passion of the exhortations to the public at large to support the policy, and the diversion of some extra resources to its effective implementation. But the basic strategy remained. This is not to deny de Valera's own special and personal commitment to the language. He was sensitive to many key aspects of language development such as the need for dictionaries, and for standardised grammar and syntax, and he took a personal interest in many aspects of Irish scholarship (for example through the founding of the Dublin Institute for Advanced Studies in 1940). Moreover, de Valera's own use of the language on public occasions was a constant reminder of its preferential status in the Irish State.

But for all that, the expected or, at least, much hoped-for breakthrough on the language front never quite materialised. Irish did not become the vernacular of the majority of the people. Indeed, within the education system the peak of committed participation in the revival policy (as measured in the number of schools and pupils being taught through Irish) was reached during the decade 1935-45. Thereafter, the language was in retreat within the system. This retreat accelerated during the sixties and seventies. For example, between 1960 and

1979 the number of Irish-medium primary schools declined from 420 to 160. A correspondingly sharp decline occurred in the secondary domain (even as participation rates in secondary education increased dramatically following the O'Malley initiative of 1967). The contraction of the Gaeltacht continued unchecked, as emigration, social dislocation and the relentless penetration of English made the surviving enclaves more and more vulnerable.

This evidence, alarming to the committed revivalist, could not be ignored. Nor was it. In fact, from the very outset, aspects of the education policy had been criticised by groups of teachers, most notably the Irish National Teachers' Organisation. They constantly complained throughout the thirties and forties that all aspects of education were being subordinated or sacrificed to the language question; that for successive Ministers for Education the only aspect of education policy which engaged their attention was the language question. It was not a case of the INTO being against the Irish language. Quite the contrary. As an organisation the INTO supported the objective of the revival of the language, and throughout the country individual national teachers were the backbone of most of the voluntary societies and organisations involved in the revival. Yet it was probably inevitable that frustration would begin to build up when persistent demands on the part of the teachers for a revaluation of policy were met, from the twenties through to the late forties, by an almost dogmatic stance of benign paternalism in the Department of Education, as successive Ministers lectured and exhorted the badly paid teachers to press on with the linguistic revolution. In an address (in Irish) to the annual congress

A market in Galway in the 1920s. To survive, the Gaeltacht areas needed prosperity. But prosperity increased the encroachment of English.

Emigration took away the young and left the old with memories.

of the INTO in Killarney, on 26 March 1940, de Valera had the following to say to the delegates: *

Níl sibh gan cúraimí eile – iad sin atá le léamh ar bhur gcuid tráth-chlár. Tá oraibh an oiread sin eolais ar a laghad do theagasc do na páistí agus a theastódh uatha i gcóir saoil na linne seo – léamh, scríobh agus áireamh a chur ar a n-eolas, ionad a n-áitreabh ar uachtar na cruinne agus buneolas ar na h-eachtraí do thug ár gcine chun áitribh sa tír seo. Tá an cuspóir mór dá raibh mé ag tagairt ar ball beag á chomhlíonadh trí athbheochan na Gaeilge, chomh fada agus is féidir sin a dhéanamh sna scoileanna.

Ní gá dom a theacht thar tábhacht an chuspóra sin. Is beag má tá duine ar bith in bhur measc gur gá a chur ar a shúile dó nach féidir náisiún slán a dhéanamh dínn mura n-éirí linn ceangal cóir a dhéanamh idir sinne agus ár sinsear romhainn.

Is é an rud is mó a theastaíonn uaim a shárú inniu oraibh, an géar-ghá atá le críochniúlacht san iarracht.

However, it wasn't simply frustration with the curriculum and other aspects of the policy in the schools which produced disappointment and criticism. Despite some advances in the Civil Service, by the thirties it was patently obvious that the language was not making a dramatic breakthrough into wide areas of social life – in the world of commerce and trade, of law and local government; in the Churches and the newspapers; most of all, perhaps, in the hurly-burly of public debate in the Dáil and on the hustings. And still the exhortation continued.

Nor was it only the teachers who began to have doubts and to voice them. By the late thirties groups of language revivalists began to bestir themselves, as they realised that the existence of a sovereign Irish state did not in

174

---

* This passage is translated on page 216.

itself (as many Gaelic Leaguers had believed) guarantee
the saving of the language. The result was a rapid growth
from the late thirties in the number of new voluntary
Irish language organisations, each in its own way con-
centrating on areas of social life outside the classroom,
which the state was not servicing, or, at least, not servicing effectively. Significantly, one particular area which
attracted attention in this "second wave" of revivalism
was publishing, with the establishment of new journals,
Comhar (1942), *Feasta* (1948), and the newspaper *Inniu*
(1943); and the influential publishing house of Sáirséal
agus Dill (1945). This was an area where the intervention
of the bureaucratic state of the twenties and thirties had
not been notably enlightened. For example, some of the
small company of writers equipped to develop a lively
vernacular literature in Irish (Séamas MacGrianna for
instance) spent valuable years chained to An Gúm trans-
lating into Irish thousands of pages from some of the
classics of English literature – and much that was far from
being classic. It is possible to detect the good intent
behind this extraordinary enterprise – at a minimum it
provided a job at home for those who could write in Irish
– but the utilisation of such literary talent to provide Irish
translations of *A Tale of Two Cities* or *Three Men in a Boat*
for a society almost totally literate in English, seems in
retrospect an enterprise mistaken to the point of
absurdity.

For the best part of forty years exhortation rather than
revaluation continued to dictate the government's response to all questioning of the language policy. In the
face of the evidence this was a dangerous line to take. In
time, it led to disillusionment and plain cynicism. The
ritual use of a smattering of Irish on official occasions or
in public speeches, while frequently meant to indicate

respect for the language, was ultimately counter-productive, leading, as it did, to charges of opportunism, hypocrisy and cant. These charges – though not without substance in some individual cases – were, in general, simplistic and wide of the mark. The fact was, that as the rhetoric of "national aspiration" atrophied, it became progressively more difficult, even in the face of all the evidence, to admit to doubt (let alone failure) on the revival strategy. Ritual genuflection before the historic aspiration came to do service for the deed itself. Among public figures, the "cúpla focal" in Irish as a prelude to the substantial statement in English may have sufficed to indicate that the speaker's "heart was in the right place", but it wasn't the location of the heart but the activity of the tongue which was the problem in the language revival policy. The sentimental, maudlin desire for virtue came to be substituted for the extremely cerebral reappraisal of resources and options involved in any serious exercise in socio-cultural development. Incredibly, it was not until 1956 that the geographical limits of the Gaeltacht were officially defined (and then incorrectly), and a further decade was to elapse before a major reassessment of the language revival policy was undertaken by the state. By this time, of course, the entire context of social and cultural, no less than economic, development in Ireland was being completely transformed. The old gods had lost their magic. On the language issue, the essence of the de Valera creed – that what was required was something approaching a mass conversion through individual revelation – found little favour in the Lemass rhetoric of growth rates, targets, projections and, most importantly, results. None of de Valera's successors as Taoiseach (nor as President, with the exception of Cearbhall Ó Dálaigh) had as deep an attachment, indeed, devotion to the language as de Valera himself had. And, yet, personal devotion had not sufficed in de Valera's attempts to revive Irish. It remained to be seen if those of lesser faith could do any better.

If de Valera's republic was not Irish-speaking, neither was it a contented small-farmer society, holding, feeding and providing adequate employment for its population. Here the figures almost speak for themselves.

Firstly, the state continued to lose population through a constant haemorrhage of emigrants from the twenties to the sixties, with a brief respite during 1945-51.

Secondly, the reduced society which remained became progressively more urbanised, as rural depopulation continued uninterrupted:

Town and Rural Population in 26 Counties
(in thousands)

	town	*rural*
1926	959	2,013
1936	1,099	1,869
1946	1,161	1,794
1951	1,272	1,688
1956	1,287	1,611
1961	1,307	1,512
1966	1,417	1,465

These figures reveal the general trend, but boundary changes dictate that they must be amended for different years before exact comparisons can be made (see James Meenan, *The Irish Economy since 1922*, Liverpool 1970, pp. 184 – 5).

Thirdly, within this reduced rural community, de Valera's beloved small farmer counted for less and less as time went on:

Number and Sizes of Holdings in 26 Counties, 1910–61

Sizes of Holdings (in Acres)	1910	1931	1939	1949	1960
1–5	48,274	30,687	27,686	26,360	23,312
5–15	115,882	73,362	67,417	62,423	47,476
15–30	103,547	90,364	90,765	86,983	73,295
30–50	58,728	62,267	62,478	64,453	62,056
50–100	48,524	49,873	49,966	51,287	54,209
100–200	20,486	21,081	21,021	21,772	22,884
Above 200	8,602	7,949	7,399	7,270	7,076
Total Holdings Over 1 Acre	**404,043**	**335,583**	**326,732**	**318,548**	**290,308**

Fourthly, agriculture accounted for a constantly diminishing percentage of the labour force in the half century after 1922:

One legacy of partition was that 93 per cent of the Irish Free State was Catholic. With such dominance arguments about minority rights and pluralism if voiced at all were lost in a sea of figures. Priests attend funeral of Archbishop Walsh in Dublin in 1921.

Numbers Engaged in Agriculture in the 26 Counties (in thousands)

	1926	1936	1946	1951	1961
Employers and workers on their own count	269	260	252	236	211.7
Relatives assisting	264	244	204	171	108
Employees	122	113	124	97	56.6
Totals	**655**	**617**	**580**	**504**	**376.3**

The social reality behind these stark figures is massively documented and unrelievedly depressing. A conservative society with an inexorably declining population, relentlessly decanting its potential constituency of dissent into the emigrant ship; with low marriage rates, high average marriage age and a higher percentage of unmarried ageing bachelors and spinsters than any society in western Europe. The abiding literary images of the chronic melancholy and lassitude of mind and body which enveloped this society are those of Patrick Kavanagh's Paddy Maguire, the ageing celibate bachelor racked by loneliness and sexual frustration on the stony grey soil of Monaghan, or of William Trevor's dutiful Bridie and her tribe of long-suffering sisters, drooping lilies of the damp ballrooms of romance throughout rural Ireland, hopelessly remembering "the youths who'd danced with her .... in their Saturday-night blue suits", but who had "later disappeared into the town, or to Dublin or Britain, leaving behind them those who became the middle-aged bachelors of the hills"; or indeed, the memorable portrait of the tangled and contradictory emotions of the prospective emigrant in Brian Friel's *Philadelphia Here I Come*.

The obsession with inheritance and succession which dominated the rural society of peasant proprietors extended far beyond the farmyard gate. The sacred principles of "service and seniority" governed many areas of Irish social life. On the order of seniority drawn by lot in their first year in Maynooth depended the promotion order of the curates of Ireland. Within the Civil Service the "seniority principle" acted as a powerful check on any dangerous impulses to recruit or promote on the basis of special skills or proven aptitudes. In department stores, drapers' assistants served out their time to become charge

With no prospects of earning a livelihood outside farming, inheritance became an obsession. Marriage often only became possible when aged parents died. This resulted in late marriages and in many cases non-marriage.

hands, and charge hands waited in hope of elevation to the ranks of buyers. Indeed, even in the highly protected manufacturing sector of the thirties, the family firm often gave clear preference to the obligations of family succession rather than to the dictates of managerial competence.

If this society were imbued with any Christian principles, then we might reasonably assume that its most appropriate and most needed Christian virtues were those of fortitude and resignation. This should not sound like an accusation. There was much social harmony and public virtue in a society with an exceptionally low crime rate. However, the harmony and deference, the relative complacency of the ideological context, depended ultimately on the extraordinary accident of emigration, on the state's continuing ability to export a sizeable section of its young population.

Yet, to see the de Valera era as an unbroken interlude of deep social torpor would be to settle for only part of the story. The dominant rhetoric of *intégrisme* current in the first fifty years of the sovereign Irish state raised fundamental and potentially disturbing questions about the nature of the 26-counties: specifically, on the nature of Church-State relations, the credibility of its republican pretensions and the seriousness of its professed aspiration for "the re-integration of the national territory".

In any assessment of Church-State relations in modern Ireland the point which has to be emphasised again and again is the extraordinary homogeneity, in terms of religious loyalty, of the 26-county state established in 1922. Roughly 93 percent of the population were Catholics; and not merely (as in parts of continental Europe) nominal Catholics, but overwhelmingly committed, well-disciplined, practising Catholics. Through historical development, the education system was almost entirely denominational, and for almost a century before 1922 the priest had been a crucial element (in many instances *the* crucial element) in virtually all forms of collective social or political action among the Catholic community.

There was no gulf between the people and the Church in Ireland. The priests, nuns and brothers came from the people and served God through the people. There existed no significant anti-clerical group as found in other European Catholic countries.

When, therefore, we speak of "the influence of the Catholic Church" on the modern Irish state, we are not merely referring to the powerful influence of the Catholic hierarchy, operating (and operating most effectively) as a major "interest group" in society; we are, rather, referring to an all-embracing value-system, a comprehensive body of ethical moral and social teaching. It is against this background that we must assess the development of what has often been described as a substantially confessional state in the 26 counties from the 1920s to the 1950s. Here again there is a tendency to see

Éamon de Valera's own deep and simple piety, his devotion to his Church and obedience to it in faith and morals, scarcely need emphasising. Yet it would be absurd to ascribe the dominant ethos of the decades after 1922 to the personal views and habits of one man. Éamon de Valera greeting Cardinal Agagianian in 1961.

de Valera as the creator rather than as the embodiment (in somewhat dramatic form) of the spirit of the age.

De Valera's own deep and simple piety, his devotion to his Church and obedience to it in faith and morals, scarcely need emphasising; likewise his somewhat severe and ascetic views and habits – an abstemious man himself, he was deeply suspicious of the evils of drink and gambling, and indeed any suggestion of "excess" – amounting to what one biographer describes as "puritanical morality". But it would be absurd to ascribe the dominant ethos of the decades after 1922 simply to the personal views and habits of one man, or indeed of any group of political leaders. The fact remains that, with very few exceptions, the political élite of the de Valera era was drawn from a largely homogeneous Catholic society and was broadly reflective of that society's values and standards.

This was clearly reflected in the social legislation of the twenties and thirties, culminating in the 1937 Constitution. But, as with the language question, what is remarkable is the continuity in intent and strategy between the twenties and the late forties. The legislative instruments of social control forged in the twenties are easily summarised:

1. The Censorship of Films Act 1923 – establishing a film censor with power to cut/ban films "subversive of public morality".
2. The Intoxicating Liquor Act 1924 – reducing the hours of opening of public houses.
3. The Intoxicating Liquor Act 1927 – reducing the number of licensed premises.
4. The legislative ban on divorce within the state, 1925.
5. Censorship of Publications Act 1929 – establishing a Censorship Board with power to ban books deemed

indecent or obscene in tendency, and also making it an offence to circulate literature advocating birth-control.

The advent of Fianna Fáil to office in 1932 saw an intensification of this confessional thrust in certain key areas of social life. Indeed, it was as if the erstwhile excommunicants of the civil war years were especially anxious to re-establish their credentials with the Catholic Church. They were going to trump the Cosgrave government in their attention to orthodox Catholic social teaching, especially in the areas of family, marriage, parental authority and sexual morality. The central, controlling idea of protecting people from "occasions of sin" echoes as clearly from the rhetoric of Dáil debates as from the lenten pastorals of the bishops. For example:

1933: A tax on imported daily newspapers sought to check the flow of English newspapers into the country.

1935: The Criminal Law Amendment Act prohibited the sale and distribution of contraceptives.

1935: The Public Dance Halls Act sought to regulate dances throughout the country by making it necessary to obtain a licence to hold public dances. The intention here was to curb the country dances in houses or at crossroads and, above all, to make public entertainment of this kind more amenable to supervision.

Then in 1937 came the new Constitution, the "coping-stone" of the constitutional and confessional developments which had been going on for fifteen years.

The 1937 Constitution contained a number of crucial articles relating to fundamental rights. In addition to reciting the usual freedoms associated with the liberal democratic system (i.e. freedom of person, equality be-

The government in the 1920s reduced the number of licensed premises and the hours of opening. They could not do much about the public demand for alcohol.

fore the law, freedom of expression subject to public order and morality, etc.), these articles also proclaimed the *family* as "the natural primary and fundamental unit group of Society and as a moral institution possessing inalienable and imprescriptible rights, antecedent and superior to all positive law". The *family* was the primary and natural educator of the child. The institution of marriage was given constitutional protection, and divorce was prohibited. Furthermore, the Constitution (Article 41) stressed the domestic and family role of women, recognising that "by her life within the home, woman gives to the State a support without which the common good cannot be achieved". Accordingly, the state undertook to "endeavour to ensure that mothers shall not be obliged by economic necessity to engage in labour to the neglect of their duties in the home". Further articles guaranteed the rights to private property, conditional on their being reconciled with the exigencies of the common good; and, while the state's obligation to protect the weaker sections of society and its right to intervene to prevent monopolies detrimental to the common good were both proclaimed, the main economic role of the state was to "favour, and, where necessary, supplement private initiative in industry and commerce".

Finally, the articles on *religion*, in addition to the guarantees of freedom of conscience and the free profession and practice of religion subject to public order and morality, contained a clause (not present in the 1922 Constitution) which was to cause much discussion in the decades which followed. This was Article 44.1. in which the state recognised "the special position of the Holy Catholic Apostolic and Roman Church as the guardian of the Faith professed by the great majority of the citizens", while also recognising the other religious

The cinema was, and continued to be, one of the most popular forms of mass entertainment. Censorship was very strict. This illustration is taken from a British Paramount newsreel of 1944 which reported in a hostile manner on Éire's neutrality.

Éamon de Valera was enormously popular. Despite a dull voice and a habit of speaking at great length on whatever topic concerned him he always attracted huge crowds. Amongst his supporters he was almost worshipped. De Valera speaking in Carlow in 1948.

denominations existing in Ireland at the date of the coming into effect of the new Constitution. The Constitution acknowledged Almighty God as the source of all authority.

Undoubtedly the 1937 Constitution was, in many ways, a document of its time. Its suspicion of the intrusive powers of the state, of the dangers of its encroachment on individual rights, must be seen in the context of the rise of totalitarian regimes (of the Right and the Left) in Europe during the inter-war years. But it is also a document which clearly reflects major elements of Catholic social thinking current at the time. This isn't surprising. In drafting the Constitution de Valera had consulted with the leaders of most of the religious denominations within the state; but the main sources of advice and inspiration were Catholic. We know that he studied the papal encyclicals (notably *Rerum Novarum* of Leo XIII and *Quadragesimo Anno* of Pius XI) and the writings of two articulate Catholic professors at Maynooth, Dr. Lucey and Dr. Browne (afterwards bishops of Cork and Galway, respectively). We know also that he received plenty of advice from the Jesuit, Fr Cahill of Milltown Park, and that he was particularly well-briefed on Catholic social thinking by the young Fr John Charles McQuaid (afterwards Archbishop of Dublin). The final product gave general satisfaction to the leaders of the Catholic Church in Ireland (and indeed in Rome), though the Constitution continued to be criticised by a minority of the Catholic laity in Ireland on the grounds that it was not sufficiently Catholic.

The Catholic hierarchy were almost to a man hostile to Fianna Fáil in 1932. When Archbishop Byrne of Dublin died in 1940 John Charles McQuaid was a surprise choice. He had been a close advisor of Éamon de Valera for a number of years.

John Charles McQuaid was a tough able archbishop. Despite his long association with Éamon de Valera the two clashed in private several times as Éamon de Valera was emphatic in separating Church and State.

The 1937 Constitution, and indeed the general corpus of legislation relating to public morals, censorship, etc., raise some basic questions about the nature of the Irish state after 1922, and particularly about its sensitivity to the rights of minorities and the credibility of its declared aspirations for reunification with the North.

In the first place, the authoritarian and censorious atmosphere brought with it a great deal of frustration and of petty tyranny. The legislative instruments of social control were no "empty formula". The mood of censorship was quite pervasive: it dictated not only what went on the shelves of local libraries or bookstores, but also what plays might grace the stages of local halls when presented by the local dramatic societies; or what topics might be discussed on the national radio service (and, at times, in what accents). Not all of this takes on a comic glow in retrospect. One of the saddest indictments of the censorious mentality of the period is the picture of the Tailor Buckley and Anstey kneeling contritely on the floor of their house in Guagán Barra, while their innocent and uninhibited book was burnt in front of them.

In view of the dominance of Catholic social thinking in the framing of the state's social policy from the twenties to the forties it is tempting to enquire whether there was any substance at all to the official republican rhetoric of these years, with its invocation of Tone and Davis and their message of cultural and religious pluralism. Was there any basis to the claim that the state was neutral

The Eucharistic Congress of 1932 witnessed a spontaneous popular enthusiasm for the Catholic Church in Ireland. This obviously eased some of the difficulties for the hierarchy facing a new government made up of men the most of whom had been excommunicated by the hierarchy a decade earlier for their opposition to the Treaty.

Fair day in Cashel, 1945. Ireland emerged from the war isolated economically and culturally. In the post war years there were plentiful signs of a widespread, uneven but accelerating collapse of belief in the dominant social and cultural slogans which had been the orthodoxies of the first twenty-five years of the state.

between the different denominations? Was its claim that minorities were fairly treated merely cant? Some of de Valera's bitterest critics occasionally asserted that this was indeed the case (for example, Seán Ó Faoláin). But the picture was a complex one, full of paradoxes and contradictions.

De Valera might insist that "the special recognition of the Catholic Church" was no more than the acknowledgement of a sociological fact, but others saw it as in some way an indication of the primacy of the Catholic element within the social whole. This impression was probably reinforced by the presence of Catholic bishops at such public occasions of social endeavour as the opening of new housing estates; or by the presence of government ministers at Catholic ceremonial occasions such as the special anniversaries of saints. Two incidents which aptly illustrate the impact of private belief on public politics were, on the one hand, the great Eucharistic Congress of 1932 where civic and state dignitaries were prominent in the religious celebration, and, on the other hand, the extraordinary funeral of Douglas Hyde in 1949 where leading political figures (including the Taoiseach of the day) remained outside the door of the Protestant church in which the funeral service of the former President was taking place. Again, the fact that successive Irish governments reaffirmed the loyalty of "the Irish people" to successive popes (and this was as true in 1948 under the Coalition government as it was under de Valera) seemed further evidence that, unconsciously in many cases, there was a widespread assumption among the political leaders that "the Irish people" and "the Catholic people" were interchangeable terms.

Yet this is not the whole story. De Valera was scrupulous in observing the full courtesies of ceremony (and in consultations on state business) in his dealings with minority Church leaders. The first head of state under the new constitution was a Protestant, and members of minority denominations were positively prized within the main political parties. Again, de Valera's consistent generosity towards Trinity College (and his affection for it) wasn't entirely due to his justified suspicion of the Cumann na nGaedheal cave in the academic corridors of Earlsfort Terrace. It also rested on an instinctive historic sense of reconciliation and ecumenism. Finally, for one minority group, the acknowledgement of their freedoms in the 1937 Constitution was a beacon of enlightenment in the dark thirties: this, of course, was the Jewish community.

And what of the minorities themselves? How comfortable were they in the new state? Did they make any complaint of the dominant ethos?

The Protestant communities within the Free State had, of course, suffered considerable trauma in the turmoil of 1919-22. Understandably they approached the new state after 1922 with caution. With few exceptions, the years after 1922 were in fact years of political quietism for southern Protestants. They kept a low profile. They were still, by and large, a community anchored in the economically well-off sector of Irish society in the new state, and were anxious to hold their property, place and position.

While ideologically some southern Protestants felt uncomfortable with key elements of the dominant values in the de Valera state – republican-separatist in political aspiration, Catholic in ethos, and, officially at least, Gaelic in cultural inspiration – yet they found, in practice, no intolerable obstacles to their right to go their own way. They largely retained their contacts (social and educational, for example) in Britain, and certainly there is little evidence to suggest that in operational terms they found the restrictive confessional laws (for example, on divorce and contraception) an intolerable burden on their normal lives. Indeed, the major worry to the southern Protestant community, that of their declining numbers, had less to do with any policies of the state than with the entirely Church problem of Catholic teaching in relation to mixed marriages. Problems in the marriage and reproduction rate (and emigration) were a bigger threat to the Protestant community in the Free State than confessional articles in de Valera's constitution. In any case, with a few notable exceptions, the leaders of Protestant opinion within the Free State were not the most vocal public critics of development in social policy within the Irish state in the de Valera era.

The same, by and large, can be said of the dominant Labour voice of these years. Fianna Fáil's early radical cutting edge – which produced initiatives in social welfare provisions and in public housing in the thirties – effectively eclipsed the official Irish Labour Party, racked as it was during these decades by internal division. Generally as staunchly Catholic in direction and rhetoric as either Cumann na nGaedheal or Fianna Fáil, the Irish Labour Party in the turbulent thirties had one brief, excited flirtation with class rhetoric (when their constitution inserted the old Connolly slogan of the Workers' Republic), but, under pressure from worried Catholics within the trade union movement, this indiscretion was quickly expunged. The party's instincts remained humane; its energies directed towards the amelioration of hardship and the improvement of the living standards of the working-classes. But it offered no fundamental challenge to the dominant ideology in the state. For the rest, the socialist or radical critique of the Irish state's social conservatism (and its social failures on such issues as emigration, land redistribution, etc.) came largely from minority socialist republican groups, sniping from the margins of Irish political life.

In fact, the most forceful criticism of the new state's evolving conservative Catholic ethos came from a highly articulate group of writers and artists, who kept up a constant criticism of censorship, philistinism, complacent insularity, intolerance and hypocrisy, from the twenties through to the fifties. Yeats and AE had been foremost in discharging this function in the twenties, and Yeats also articulated a version of Protestant indignation with confessional developments (such as the divorce ban in 1925) considerably more trenchant than anything coming from the official voices of southern Protestantism. Many of those writers who took up this role of public critics of the state were themselves of Catholic, republican and Gaelic background (for example, Ó Faoláin, Frank O'Connor and Peadar O'Donnell); some of them indeed had been participants in the heady days of the independence struggle prior to the establishment of the Free State. Others felt unable to share in the uncritical reverence for the rural ideal which dominated the de Valera version of the authentic Ireland. All of these writers, in their different ways, were writing out of a profound disillusionment with the Irish state; a sense of betrayal greeted its tired slogans, its timorous address to social problems, its manifest failure to seriously tackle those heroic tasks of state-building for which it had been founded and to which its leaders continued to proclaim their unswerving commitment. Certainly some of this criticism was unmeasured, took little account of many of the difficulties facing successive governments in the economic sphere, and generally underestimated what had actually been achieved (for example, the maintenance of a competitive, multi-party democratic system in the highly dangerous decades of the inter-war years in Europe). But this persistent criticism, voiced in a succession of periodicals, from the *Irish Statesman* to *The Bell*, represented a crucial constituency of dissent within Ireland in the second quarter of the century.

The war years undoubtedly accentuated the social and cultural isolation of the Irish state (though the growing number of "wireless sets" from the thirties ensured that this insularity was never total). However, in the postwar years there are plentiful signs of a widespread, uneven, but accelerating collapse of belief in the dominant social and cultural slogans which had been the orthodoxies of the first twenty-five years of the state. The moulds of dogma and certainty began to crack, though at an uneven rate, and with, as yet, no certainty as to what would replace them.

With the successive economic crises of the fifties, and the massive emigration of that decade, the very viability of a sovereign Irish state came under question. In this context, the completion of the long constitutional gestation of the state into its pure republican form seemed something of an anti-climax, the principal effect of which seemed to be the further distancing of the North as a separate political entity.

Within the Republic the years between 1946 and 1959 were years of transition. The high turnover of governments was one indication of the restiveness of the electorate. The evidence from the schools and the examination of the Gaeltacht's position in the mid-fifties were

The symbols of post-Independence Ireland – the round tower, the harp, the wolfhound, the donkey with creels of turf – began to be replaced. In some cases an accommodation could be found.

Despite growing urbanisation from the 1950s onwards political issues and debate tended to remain linked to the past.

straws in the wind of the growing doubts about the language strategy. In Church-State relations, the protracted controversies over the state's responsibilities in health (which spanned the years from 1947 to 1953, reaching a climax in the Mother and Child controversy of 1951), marked a watershed; from the fifties the state's initiatives in social policy (even in the crucial area of education) became less and less open to the charge that they were "confessional" in character.

Out of the doubting, despairing fifties, with Irish society showing alarming signs of major social dislocation, it was inevitable that new questions would be asked. It was certain that there would be a desire for a new coherent version of why and to what purpose there ought to be a sovereign Irish state at all; and one, moreover, which would frame its *raison d'être* not in the obsessive language of obligation to the dead generations, but rather in terms which acknowledged a primary obligation to the living generation. There was, of course, a generation shift taking place in Irish society. Increasingly from the late forties the generation which had founded the state was handing over the reins of control to a new generation in many areas of Irish life. By 1947 De Valera was sixty-five years of age. He had been a long time at the top. His public life had still a long term to run, but on all sides the younger generation were moving into place to take over from the revolutionary generation. Lemass, despite his years, was the midwife of the new ethos which began to inform Irish life and the Irish state during the sixties and seventies. External factors were crucial to the transition. The international economic climate was favourable to the Whitaker initiatives in economic planning from the late fifties. The opening up of a public debate on a wide range of social and cultural issues and standards was powerfully stimulated by the impact of television, growing from the BBC spill-over of the fifties to the launching of the Irish national service in the early sixties. Within the Catholic community itself there were important shifts of perception and opinion in the aftermath of Vatican II, with a greater awareness of, and sensitivity to, the rights of other denominations, especially those on one's own doorstep. Rising population and economic expectations produced a decisive shift in public attitudes. Dissent was no longer for export only. Increased travel opportunities (the result of growing affluence) encouraged intellectual curiosity and cultural relativism. Inevitably, the new mood carried its own risks. Iconoclasm unsettles the tribe of believers. The aggressive new vocabulary of economic expansion, growth rates and gross national product was a welcome change from sentimental fatalism, but it needed to be tempered with some version of equity and compassion if social cohesion were to hold. Achieving this balance – between real growth and fair distribution – was to prove a most difficult matter indeed.

By the sixties, however, there could be no ignoring the public and formal signs of ideological reappraisal. In 1966 (a significant anniversary) a commission was established to review the Constitution. Already a commission was at work reviewing the language revival strategy. By this time the man in the Park – the Chief – came more and more to seem like a figure from the past. The age of de Valera had clearly run its course.

Chapter 6

Parting Shots

In the course of preparation of the television series "The Age of de Valera", some sixty interviews were recorded with people who had met Éamon de Valera at various stages during his long life. Over twenty hours of interviewing were recorded. Inevitably, given the constraints of broadcasting time in any television series, most of what is recorded is not transmitted. The untransmitted material is deposited in the RTE Libraries, hopefully to be of use some day to either future programme makers or historians. What follows is a somewhat arbitrary and unrepresentative sample of some of the most interesting things said in interview.

Peter Feeney
Producer
The Age of de Valera

Parting Shots

Peadar O'Donnell, writer and radical socialist

"Eamon de Valera has passed on into Irish history. Like all men who have achieved that kind of eminence certain myths are and will continue to be attached to his name. Amongst all these the one that I think is very unfair is the suggestion that he was responsible for the Civil War. That simply is not true. You may as well blame a rainy day on the weather forecaster as blame de Valera for the Civil War."

Seán MacEntee, former Tanaiste and cabinet colleague of Éamon de Valera

"The 1937 Constitution was a product of its age. It reflected the social thinking of the mass of the Irish people. Nothing was imposed in that Constitution. Everything was firstly discussed in the Dáil and then put to the Irish people. It reflects the general opinion of the mass of the Irish people."

Lord Garner, former Head of the British Diplomatic Service

"One's bound to say that everybody on the British side who had dealings with Éamon de Valera, even Maffey who got very close to him, and certainly MacDonald and Chamberlain who negotiated with him, found him austere, rigid, obstinate and very much with a one-track mind. There was no doubt that he was obsessed with the undesirability of partition and I can understand that. But he did press, he never let go. He was like a dog with a bone, he would always come back to it."

Maurice Moynihan, former Secretary of the Department of the Taoiseach

"I think Éamon de Valera was a man of great moral rectitude which seemed to me to be a fundamental thing in his character. I think he was skilful as a politician and a negotiator. He was also courageous and not capable of being over-awed by anybody, however powerful, that he might come into contact with. He was a man of warm affections and tolerant human feelings."

Kevin Boland, former Fianna Fáil government Minister

"Fianna Fáil was the party of the small man both in urban areas and in rural areas and I know my father always put the changing character of Fianna Fáil down to the first big subscription that they got. I think shortly after they came into government a cheque arrived in the Fianna Fáil office from a prominent Cumann na nGaedheal supporter for £500."

Jack Lynch, Former Taoiseach

"As Taoiseach Eamon de Valera always insisted on very thorough and comprehensive argument on any issue. In fact, cabinet meetings used to last then almost twice as long as they did subsequently under Mr. Lemass. I always felt though that he had his mind pretty well made up in advance about what kind of a decision he reached, and, not always, but invariably he succeeded in having that decision reached."

Parting Shots

Dermot Foley, Librarian in Ennis in the 1930s and 40s

"His visits to Clare, in my opinion – again a personal view – were more like the bishop's visitations or coming down to give Confirmation and he was treated like a bishop in that way. I don't object at all. But if de Valera had asked the question one day – 'I'd like to see this particular school or have you a library?' If he had walked over to the library to have a look at it, he would have done my scheme and those things I was trying to do an enormous amount of good. But you see he was not an intellectual in that sense."

Rev. Ernest Gallagher, former President of the Methodist Church in Ireland

"I would say that most people in those days regarded him as a man of integrity, a devout Catholic but yet one who didn't allow himself to be dictated to, certainly politically, by the Roman Catholic Church. He took an independent stance on such matters as his attitude to Franco in Spain or the Abyssinian issue which probably weren't very popular with the Roman Catholic establishment of those days."

*Sir Ian McLennan, former British Ambassador to
Ireland*

"I suppose one of my earliest political recollections
you could say was as a small boy reading and
hearing about the troubles in 1920 and '21. The
name of Eamon de Valera was naturally extremely
prominent at that time. So he was a man with
whose name I had been familiar for a very long
time. When I first went over to Ireland I had some
trepidation as the sort of picture that I had formed
of Mr de Valera was not necessarily attractive.
When I met him first I was completely taken by him
as a personality. He is one of the few people I have
ever met whom you are convinced from the beginning that he is, was a great man, quite irrespective of what his beliefs or philosophy or politics
were."

Douglas Gageby, Editor of the Irish Times
"The interesting thing to me was that behind this
apparently austere man, and he was very austere in
many ways, was a very jolly character. He came
into the Irish Times once. We were unveiling a
plaque to Sean MacDermott in D'Olier Street. Donal
Foley and myself had Dev for about an hour and a
half, full of good stories, taking a glass of brandy
and indeed he was the last to leave."

Parting Shots

Patrick Lynch, former Professor of Political Economy

"I had the honour of working in a very humble way in Mr de Valera's private office as a civil servant and I remember one day asking him how would he label himself as a politician – was he a conservative or a liberal? He said these words did not mean anything to him at all. He would regard himself perhaps, he said, in the English language as a radical."

Patrick Shea, former Department Secretary, the Northern Ireland Civil Service

"In those years Eamon de Valera was the devil incarnate to the Unionists. He was public enemy number one. Remember he had come through the civil war and therefore he was associated with the men of violence. He was making speeches every week and every speech he made was a threat to the North of Ireland."

John Swift, former Trade Union Official

"I joined the Volunteers early in 1914 – the Dublin Third Battalion of the Volunteers. We attended drill in a hall in York Street but on Saturdays we paraded in a field in Kimmage. We met the battalion officers of course, including Eamon de Valera. He took part in the drilling of the battalion and we regarded him as a kind of remote figure. We couldn't afford to buy a uniform, but the officers could, including de Valera. I remember de Valera always came in uniform. He came on a bicycle and we thought he looked rather funny. He was a very tall man riding on a bicycle in a uniform and we had a sense of class distinction over these differences and you see, also, we got to learn that Eamon de Valera was in St Vincent de Paul. This was significant to us as we all remembered the role St Vincent de Paul played in the Larkin lockout the year before in 1913."

Brendan Malin, Political Correspondent of the Irish Press in the 1940s

"De Valera didn't overwhelm the people he met. He touched fingers with them and they regarded him as one of themselves. His name of course had a mystique to it. Above all he seemed to be able to come into complete concert with what the people wanted to do and the methods by which they proposed to do it."

Patrick Quinlan, former President Irish Agricultural Organisation Society

"Dev's idea was having a peasant population of small farmers living in what he termed frugal comfort. It's a common picture and it's largely based on too much reading of poor old Charlie Kickham's view of the pre-famine conditions in his mythical Knocknagow and you see Kickham was writing about the conditions as he imagined they would be in the 1830s. But the 1830s were known in rural Ireland as the hungry thirties. Small people in Ireland were never satisfied. They had no reason to be satisfied, they were living in misery."

Lady Penelope Aitken, daughter of Lord Rugby, the British Representative to Ireland during the War

"Neutrality was very popular. De Valera's policy was very popular. And of course people had no news. There was no editorial comment and nothing was ever written to offend Germany or Great Britain. So people didn't know very much about anything. If I was to stick my neck out I would say there was a groundswell of feeling, there were a lot of people who liked to think that Great Britain was going to have a really bad kick, but they didn't want Germany to win the war."

Lord Longford, biographer, historian and lifelong friend of Eamon de Valera

"I do regard him as the greatest statesman that I have ever encountered and I think statesmen have to be ambiguous at certain times. When I say ambiguous I don't mean that they are setting out to mislead anybody. Rather that when an issue cannot be settled then you've got to find words which enable the issue to be left unsettled for the time being. Therefore you have got to find words which satisfy both sides."

List of Illustrations

The copyright source of each photograph,
where applicable, is indicated in *Italic* type

Chapter 1   Biographical Profile

Chapter 2   De Valera and Political Sovereignty: The Idée Fixe

List of Illustrations

Blueshirt Children *(Cork Examiner)*

Éamon de Valera during 1933 Election *(British Movietone Newsreel)*

Éamon de Valera leaving for Anglo Irish Talks, 1932 *(Independent Newspapers)*

Éamon de Valera in London, 1932 *(BBC Hulton Picture Library)*

Douglas Hyde Inauguration, 1938 *(Independent Newspapers)*

Army March Past GPO, 1941 *(Independent Newspapers)*

Inter-Party Cabinet, 1948 *(Irish Press)*

Fianna Fáil Cabinet, 1951 *(Irish Press)*

Éamon de Valera & Charles de Gaulle in 1969 *(G. A. Duncan)*

Chapter 3   Fractured Sovereignty: Partition

Bangor in early 1900's *(Ulster Folk & Transport Museum)*

Orange Parade in Belfast *(Ulster Folk & Transport Museum)*

Man Pasting Election Poster *(BBC Hulton Picture Library)*

Arrest of Éamon de Valera, 1924 *(Gaumont Newsreel from Visnews Library)*

High Street Belfast in early 1900's *(Ulster Folk & Transport Museum)*

Harland & Wolff, Belfast in early 1900's *(Ulster Folk & Transport Museum)*

Altar on O'Connell Bridge during Eucharistic Congress *(Independent Newspapers)*

Chapter 4   The Price of Independence

Chapter 5 De Valera and the Irish People

Cottage in Donegal *(Ulster Folk & Transport Museum)*

Girl at Euston Station *(BBC Hulton Picture Library)*

Children in Donegal *(G. A. Duncan)*

Men Saving Turf, 1940 (G. A. Duncan)

Galway Market in 1920's

Old Man in Dublin 1950's *(Radio Telefís Eireann)*

Clerical Procession in Dublin, 1921 *(Keogh Collection in National Library)*

Farmer in field (1950's) *BBC Hulton Picture Library)*

Nuns in Dublin Street (1950's) *(Radio Telefís Eireann)*

Éamon de Valera greets Cardinal Agagianian, 1961 *(G. A. Duncan)*

Men Standing outside Pub *(BBC Hulton Picture Library)*

Cinema Queue in Dublin *(British Paramount newsreel in Visnews Library)*

Éamon de Valera in Carlow, 1948 *(Associated Press)*

Archbishop McQuaid in 1940 *(Irish Independent)*

Street altar, Eucharistic Congress, 1932 *(Irish Independent)*

Fair Day in Cashel (1945) *(Bord Fáilte)*

Man Loading Turf onto car *(Connaught Telegraph)*

Man Pasting Election Poster to Rock *(BBC Hulton Picture Library)*

Éamon de Valera & Frank Aiken in 1973 *(Radio Telefís Eireann)*

Éamon de Valera and Frank Aiken in 1973. A generation of political leaders was passing. Ireland was changing rapidly. Amongst those who knew Éamon de Valera well it is said that he would not have entered politics sixty years ago if the issues then were the issues of today.

Bibliographical Note

The obvious starting point in any further reading on De Valera must be the official biographies: The Earl of Longford and Thomas P. O'Neill, *Éamon De Valera* (Dublin 1970), and Tomás P. Ó Néill agus Pádraig Ó Fiannachta, *De Valera*, 2 vols. (Baile Átha Cliath 1968–1970). Earlier biographies which retain an interest are Seán Ó Faoláin, *De Valera* (London 1939), and Mary C. Bromage, *De Valera* (London 1956). A more recent short study is T. Ryle Dwyer, *Éamon de Valera* (Dublin 1980). Maurice Moynihan's (ed.) *Speeches and Statements by Éamon De Valera, 1917-73* (Dublin and New York 1980) is invaluable. General histories which can be recommended include F. S. L. Lyons, *Ireland since the Famine* (London 1971); John A. Murphy, *Ireland in the Twentieth Century* (Dublin 1975); and Terence Brown, *Ireland: A Social and Cultural History, 1922-1979* (London 1981). Special studies worth noting are James Meenan, *The Irish Economy since 1922* (Liverpool 1970); Ronan Fanning, *The Irish Department of Finance 1922-58* (Dublin 1978); E. Rumpf and A. C. Hepburn, *Nationalism and Socialism in the Twentieth Century Ireland* (Liverpool 1977); T. Ryle Dwyer, *Irish Neutrality and the U. S. A. 1939-47* (Dublin 1977); John Whyte, *Church and State in Modern Ireland* (Dublin 1971, 1980). For some recent cultural soundings the journal *The Crane Bag* (Dublin 1977-proceeding) is recommended.

This short list gives only the merest hint of the rich and fast-growing store of historical writing on twentieth century Ireland.

Translation of passage on page 174

You have other tasks, those which appear in your timetable. It is your function to equip the children with at least the minimum of qualifications required by modern life, to teach them to read, write and calculate, to show them where they live on this globe and to give them some idea of the events which led our people to settle in this country. You have the great task that I have already mentioned (knitting up the broken thread of our national tradition) being fulfilled by the revival of the Irish language, so far as it can be revived in the schools.

I do not need to stress the importance of that task. There is scarcely one amongst you who needs to be told that we cannot be a whole and healthy nation unless we establish the essential tradition linking us to those who went before us.

What I particularly want to impress on you to-day is the need for thoroughness in this enterprise.